The boy WHO LEARNED To Read

Mohamud Ege

The boy
WHO LEARNED
To Read

MEMOIRS

Cirencester

Published by Memoirs

MEMOIRS
PUBLISHING

Memoirs Books

25 Market Place, Cirencester, Gloucestershire, GL7 2NX
info@memoirsbooks.co.uk www.memoirspublishing.com

ISBN 978-1-909020-04-7

Printed in England

The boy WHO LEARNED To Read

Contents

ACKNOWLEDGEMENTS

MY FAMILY LINEAGE

In the Somali culture all men and women learn the names of their fathers and grandfathers by heart, as nothing is written. These are the names as they would be written in Somali, starting with me at the top and going back to my 17-greats-grandfather at the bottom. I do not know when he lived, but it must have been about 500 years ago! My brother Muse can recite all these by heart. We do not have surnames - I took my surname Ege from my grandfather's name, Cige in Somali.

1. Maxamud (Mohamud)
2. Aw-cali
3. Cige
4. Cilmi
5. Wacays
6. Buux
7. Caddaawe
8. Cabdalle
9. Deerayahan
10. Xasan
11. Cabdulle
12. Muse
13. Jibriil
14. Maxamed
15. Ciise
16. Muse
17. Subeer
18. Awal
19. Isxaaq
20. Bin Ahmed

ACKNOWLEDGEMENTS

I would like to thank all of those family members and friends whom I have mentioned in the book without their prior knowledge for the parts they have played in my story. There is no malicious intent in doing so from my side!

I would also like to thank to my beloved wife Nimo, who has taken every effort to look after our four lovely children during my absence while doing my locum work up and down the country and in working on the book. I would like to thank our wonderful children for their patience during my long absences from home.

I would like to thank my editor and ghostwriter Chris Newton and his partner Barbara for their hospitality in their homes when we were writing the book. This book would not have been written without Chris' encouragement and hard work. I am sure he has had a number of sleepless nights!

Chapter One

NOMAD

My English friends know me as an educated Western clinician living in a modern British home, working in a modern British hospital and sending my children to British state schools. But my original home could not have been more different. I was born in a straw hut in the hot, dry mountains of north-western Somalia, the fourth child of a family of six siblings of desert nomads.

I have worked out that I was probably born in 1956, but I never knew the date of my birth – my people did not record such things. Later on when I came to Italy I had to invent a birthday, so I chose June 26, the date when Somaliland (the unofficial state which comprises the northern west part of the country) gained its independence from British rule in 1960.

My birthplace was a hillside east of the little town of Sheikh, which is in the mountains about 70 miles south of the coastal town of Berbera. In the days when this part of Somalia was a British protectorate, Sheikh was a principal base of the British Empire. It lies on the main route through the mountain ranges in the north from Berbera to the dry and dusty town of Burao in the south.

Like most people in the region in those days, my family were nomads. We had no permanent home and no property apart from our animals. We were however quite well off compared to many of our tribe, because at one time we had about 40 goats and 50 sheep as well as two camels. We used all the animals, including the camels, for milk, clothing and meat.

The camels were our most important possession, because they were our transport – like a family car, or better, because they need neither petrol nor diesel. They are truly masters of the desert. I suppose you could say that having two meant we were like a two-car family. A good camel was much more valuable than a sheep or a goat, because life as a nomad is impossible without them.

Today, after a series of rebellions and revolutions, Somalia is one of the most lawless states in the world. Back then it was a peaceful country, but an extremely poor one. The life of the nomads of the north was desperately hard. Southern Somalia is a paradise by comparison, with greenery all the year round, but in the north it is mostly rocky scrub and desert.

Sheikh itself used to have plenty of rainfall, but much of the rest of the north is very dry. There are places where only about four inches of rain falls in a year, barely a tenth of that in the UK, and the temperature in summer can rise to 45°C (113°F) in certain places. It is only a short distance north of the equator, so there is really no summer or winter, but there is a wet season. It is known as Gu and runs from about April to June. Without it no one could survive in northern Somalia.

During Gu, life is good. There is plenty of grass for the animals and you can relax, eat well and gain your health and strength. You can breed from your livestock and sell the good ones for cash. Our livestock were exported to Saudi Arabia, especially during the Hajj period when Muslims gather in Mecca to perform their duty of Hajj and slaughter an animal. But when the dry season or Jilaal returns, the land quickly starts turning to desert and nothing can live. If you don't move quickly to a place where there has been rain your livestock start dying, and eventually you will die as well. So you have to be ready to move at short notice. We would often say a prayer for rain, which we called a roobdoon.

During the wet season Sheikh is green and beautiful, but unfortunately the scenery in the dry season is one of semi-desert or desert. Typical desert animals are found, such as horned lizards, antelopes, hedgehogs, different varieties of poisonous snakes, ostriches, foxes, hyenas, ants, scorpions and tortoises etc. The vegetation is dominated by scrub, including thorny acacia and fig trees around the dry riverbeds.

There was no way of communicating directly with other parts of the country of course, so all information came by word of mouth. We would hear rumours of rain - someone would say 'The people in the market say there is rain a hundred miles to the south' or 'My cousin has just come from Dubur, someone told him it has been raining further up the coast'. We nomads developed a great awareness of the signs of rain; we could almost smell it, even from many miles away. Immediately we knew it had been raining somewhere, however far away, there would be a race to follow it.

Our home was an aqal, a large bell-shaped hut made of straw woven on to curved wooden poles, and very easy and quick to erect and dismantle. When the time came to move we would take our aqal apart and load all the straw and poles on to the camels. Then we would load our other possessions, our bedding, clothing and cooking equipment, and set off for the place where we had heard there was rain. You might be walking for days through desert and scrub, and if it was too dry and hot your animals would start to die and you would have to leave them by the wayside. But you couldn't wait around, because if you didn't get there quickly you would arrive to find that all the best grazing was gone.

I hated constantly having to be on the move. Imagine you have just settled in a new home and think you are going to be happy there for a while, and then you wake up to see your parents packing everything on to the camels and are told you are going to have to walk two hundred miles in the heat to some place where it might - or might not - be raining. The pace was set by the camels. If you could not keep up with the camels you had to stay behind.

There was no mercy for the weak and vulnerable. We had to survive terrible hunger, thirst and lack of sleep. It was a life which soon separated the weak from the strong. If anyone was too ill or old to keep up with us we just left them behind, and everyone accepted it. You had to be tough and fit to survive; many children died young and by the time you were 40 you were an old man.

In truth it was a terrible life. We all had to grow up very early, and I don't ever remember playing or having fun, except perhaps swimming in a river. It was as if we never had a childhood.

There was one man in Sheikh who was a hundred years old, but he was very unusual. He was OK, because he had sons. If you are childless you are called a goblan, but they use the term also for people who have only girls, because girls will go to their husbands, but they believe your genes are carried through your sons. We believe God decides these things – it's your fate. You must not challenge it or complain, you may only pray. If you lose your money you just say 'God will give it to me again'. Everything is written – you can't change it. We call this qanaaca – being satisfied with what you have.

Everyone is said to have a kind of virtual book, your kitab, in which are written all your good and bad deeds. You are judged from it on your day of judgment. You must be good to others, but more than anyone else you must be good to your mum.

In our society it is accepted that you turn to others when you need help, and most people do not mind giving. If someone calls at your house needing food or shelter – a marti, we call someone like this - you cannot turn that person away, you have to let them in and look after their needs. Normally you would offer them a bed for the night, serve them whatever food you are having and send them on their way in the morning with a cup of very strong tea with lots of sugar and milk. The first cup is served very strong, the second less so, then the third and final one is quite weak.

Of course there are always some people who are not willing to pay, and we call them bakhayl – the word for people who will not give anything to anyone else. You learn to leave them alone; they are almost outside the rest of society. 'Don't bother with him' people will say. 'He is bakhayl!'

I managed to survive quite well, though I was underdeveloped because of the constant malnourishment. We would eat rice, corn and goat's milk; goat's milk does not provide a complete food and is not good for raising children. The only food item we could store was ghee, clarified butter. We would have meat only when one of our animals was slaughtered, and we did not often kill the animals because they were more valuable to us alive.

If all went well we would arrive to find it was raining as we had been told and the grass was growing, and we would find the best place to graze our animals and put our aqal back together. No one owned any of the land; it was first come first served. But if there was no rain, or not enough, we would have to keep going. You could never be sure how far you would have to walk to find a place where you could settle for a while, or how long you would be able to stay before you had to move on again. By the end of the dry season and the start of the next Gu, our ribs would be showing and we would be feeling very hungry. It was real hunger, not what people in the modern developed world think of as hunger. You might eat nothing for days. Starvation made you ill, and it could kill you.

I was the fourth in a family of six children; I had three older sisters, Mariam, Halimo and Khadija, and a younger one, Seynab. I also had a younger brother, Muse. I had a younger half-brother, Ahmed, who died young without leaving children. We were a happy family, but we did not have much fun. There was no room for fun in the nomad life.

We belonged to one of the largest tribes in Somalia, the Awal, and like most people in that part of the African continent, we were Muslims. My father was a holy man who was well known for having healing powers. He had studied the Holy Koran, the book of Islam, and used its teachings to treat people and their animals. He would do this either by reciting verses from the Koran over them or by making holy water, which we called ashar, and giving it to them to drink or to wet their animals.

I started to learn to read the Koran when I was very young. I had always wanted to learn to read and follow my father's footsteps. The Somalian tongue had no written form in those days because of the nomadic lifestyle, so there was nothing to study in our native language. But it is not easy to learn the Arabic alphabet, and my father was very strict. If I failed to pronounce a letter correctly he would cane me. The habit of caning children was not part of Somalian culture; it had been introduced into our society by teachers from other countries visiting to learn Arabic and religion. When I was caned it made me forget everything, even my name. I experienced a fear, anxiety and stress which has never left me. The purpose of caning children was to create fear to make them learn quickly, but it had the opposite effect.

The shadow of my father's discipline was to be lifted in a shocking and most unexpected way. When I was about five years old and my brother Muse was one, a dreadful thing happened. I was lying asleep one night when I was awoken by a sudden commotion. People crowded into our aqal and there was a lot of shouting. I could see one of the camels outside and thought we must be on the move again, but then I realised something was wrong with my father; he was lying on the ground, not moving. They put him on the camel and rushed him away somewhere. I could not imagine what had happened, until my mother told me that he had been bitten by a snake. There are many kinds of poisonous snakes in Somalia and suffering a snake-bite was not unusual.

My father would have been sleeping near the entrance, so the snake must have reached him first. He was very unlucky, because he absorbed a lot of poison and died immediately. The camel had been brought round to take his body into Sheikh to be buried; he could not be buried near our home because there were not enough people to dig a grave. That was one of the hard practicalities of life.

I was devastated by the death of my father, but I was also relieved because it meant an end to the difficult lessons on the Koran, and the punishments when I got it wrong. Because I was so young when he died I have no memory of what he looked like, but I will never forget his discipline and his influence.

It was soon after this that I had to undergo ritual circumcision, as happens to all Muslim boys. It was a most unpleasant and painful experience to have it done at such a late age. The medicine man removed the foreskin (the prepuce) of my private part with an old and rusty razor blade with no anaesthesia. I felt an intense pain which continued for a number of days. There were no painkillers. The wound got infected, but I carried on without antibiotics and it took a long time to heal. I was lucky not to have lost my penis.

After my father died, life became even harder. My mother had to look after the six of us on her own. She was a marvellous and very resilient woman and somehow she managed. If my father had had brothers it would have been their responsibility to look after us as their own family, but he had only two sisters. Your family were your only security in our culture; so much so that if someone is murdered, there is usually no retributional punishment as such, instead the family or tribe of the murdered person demands payment in compensation for the loss of a member of their family, and the more important the person was the more the compensation, which was usually paid in camels, because nomads have no savings.

My mother had no choice but to get married again when she could, but she did not have much choice of husband. The man she married was a distant uncle called Robleh, who already had his own children (under my religion you are allowed to have up to four wives). I hated Robleh. I knew he was only interested in my mother's property, such as it was, and I had a fierce argument with him over it. I told him that if he touched my mother I would kill him! She should never have agreed to marry him, because he made us all so unhappy. But she did, and from this marriage, my half-brother Ahmed was born.

Years later, long after my father died, my sister Halimo married Yassin Farah, the eldest son of one of my two aunts. Yassin had a shop in Burao, 40 miles from Sheikh, and I asked him to let Muse live with him, which he did.

People were kind to me when they realised I was an orphan, or agoon as we called it. They used to give me money and advice and caress me to comfort me and show their sympathy. There was a belief that by showing kindness to an orphan in this way you would be rewarded in the afterlife. For me however it was an embarrassment, and I felt they were taking advantage of me. It also made me feel inferior, a feeling I still get even today. I did not want to be patronised as someone who needed help. I wanted to make my own way in life.

My early recollection of Sheikh was that it was a prosperous city. Most of the inhabitants lived in stone-built houses and owned Lorries that carried livestock from Burao to Berbera for export to the Gulf States, especially Saudi Arabia. Equally they transported foodstuffs from Berbera to Burao. Many more were employed by the schools, but once the military government came in the trade dried up.

There was a first-class restaurant owned by a gentleman called Abdi Hassan. He was a very hardworking individual and a no-nonsense man, but I am afraid most of the inhabitants did not appreciate it. I saw him again in 1995 while in Hargeisa and talked a lot with him, which made me realise that he was someone who appreciated those who work very hard. His restaurant had a good radio which could easily pick up the Somali BBC radio. The BBC news was transmitted at 5 o'clock every evening East African time, and people used to listen together every evening. We never missed it. I can still recall vividly the devastating war between Pakistan and India in 1971 which subsequently separated what is now the new country of Bangladesh from Pakistan.

Near to where I lived in Sheikh we had a neighbour called reer (the family of) Yassin Yare. Yassin was businessman who had a large family, and I became friendly with them. In fact it was more than a friendship; they were like my own family. One of his sons, Mohamed, who now lives in Manchester with his family, used to help his father with the business, while Abdi, the more flamboyant, was a student at secondary school. His daughter, Anab Yassin, was the person who cemented my friendship with this family. It still continues today.

Playing dominoes was one of our pastimes. At times Abdi Hassan and Yassin used to play and we used to watch eagerly. Both of them were very good players. It was interesting to watch the clash of these two heavyweights, and people used to gather around - nobody was allowed to talk while they were playing. Their game used to continue for hours. I never missed their games as they were an experience to remember.

Chapter Two

SCHOOLDAYS

After my father's death we settled on the south western side of Sheikh, near a mountain called Qarasgoy. My mother would go into the town to sell milk to the traders, and it was on one of these visits that she bumped into a distant relative called Abdillahi Yassin.

Abdillahi was a wise and intelligent man. Although he too lived the life of the nomad, he had settled his children in the town in order to educate them. He had been close to my late father, and felt sorry for the situation we were now in. He urged my mother to bring me to the town so that I could go school.

My mother understood the value of learning, and she could have sent all her children to school. Her decision to send only me to school was not discrimination between boys and girls; it was just that she considered that as the elder boy I was the most suitable to go away from home to study. So in about 1963, when I was about nine years old, she acted on Abdullah's advice and I was sent to Sheikh. I had no money of course, only the clothes I stood up in.

I saw my mother only rarely after that. In our culture the idea of being homesick or missing someone was quite alien. You just went where you had to go and managed without complaining. Of course like any young child I missed my mother terribly and was very lonely, but I could not expect anyone else to worry about my loneliness.

Sheikh owes a great deal to the British, because when it was a British protectorate they built three schools there; a primary school, an intermediate (junior) and a secondary school. It also had a new hospital, which was being built by the Russians at the time I was a child there. The construction of the hospital was a blessing to the residents of Sheikh, as it offered them an opportunity to work and earn money.

I could not walk all the way there from home, so I moved to Sheikh to live. At first I lived with a distant, a lady called Cutiya. The word cutiya means 'limp' in Somali, and she got the name because she had a deformity to her left leg and limped slightly. Every time we used her name it was like calling someone 'Cripple', but she did not seem to mind.

Cutiya lived in a one-room hut with no beds, no toilet and no shower. In the morning I had to walk down to a nearby valley to relief myself. There was nothing to clean myself with but pebbles and sticks.

Three of us slept on a large piece of rush matting on a concrete floor. There was no bedding, and in the colder months of December, January and February I would shiver all through the night. Each morning when I got up my body was imprinted with the pattern of the rush matting. But I was in no position to complain about the situation, as it was more comfortable than my previous life. In fact I was grateful to be there. My motivation to succeed and make something of myself in life was very strong.

My food was one daily meal of lahooh, a kind of plain pancake, and sometimes I did not even get that. Hunger was a constant companion. Fortunately I got talking one day to a very kind man who knew me and my family. He gave me a little money every month when he collected his salary, so I was sometimes able to buy extra food or sweets. It was at the time when Sheikh Hospital was being built. I never knew the man's name, and when the building work finished he disappeared. I suspect he was a member of the monkey tribe, my tribe. I never saw him again.

There was no play, no recreation. The nearest thing we could do to having fun was to go and play in a tog, a dry riverbed, or swim in a well.

My education took place in a small mosque which provided nursery-level education. The mosque had one room where daily prayers took place. It was surrounded by a fence made of dried sticks. Our education took place in the open air, in a corner of this fence. I started to learn the Arabic alphabet and a few verses of the Koran to start with. In the afternoon when my lessons were over I would go into the mosque to sleep, because it was more peaceful and comfortable than the hut.

On the right of the mosque stood a big tree which provided shade for people waiting for prayer to begin. Each day a handful of elderly and middle-aged men attended the five daily prayer sessions. One day while the men were waiting for the midday prayer session to start, I climbed the tree. The imam of the mosque was an elderly man whose name was Hajji Yusuf (the word Hajji denoted that he attended the yearly Muslim pilgrimage in Saudi

Arabia, which lies north of Somalia across the Gulf of Aden). His mobility was not good, so he used to walk with a stick.

When Hajji Yusuf saw me at the top of the tree he became very angry. He came up to me and hit me very hard on my right ankle with his stick. My bones were not broken, but I sustained a large bruise which stopped me going to the nursery for two weeks. My leg was very painful. The hospital in Sheikh was not built at that time and there were no doctors or nurses available, so I did not receive any medical attention. There were no over-the-counter painkillers either.

There was only one other pupil there, a boy who shared the same name as my brother, Muse. We had great difficulty in doing our homework at night because there was no light except for a dim paraffin (kerosene) lamp.

Sheikh had more rainfall than the surrounding hills and it was often wet. This meant my shoes very soon wore out. Imported shoes were not available, so we had to have shoes made locally from animal skin. There was a famous shoemaker in the town, Mr Ballase, who made shoes by shaping treated goatskin. He had no machines, but he was clever enough with his hands to make shoes to fit everyone. The disadvantage of goatskin shoes was that they could not withstand the wet weather and the rocky roads, and wore out quickly. It took a long time to raise the money for another pair, and a long time to have them made. Mr Ballase would tell you that he would finish the shoes tomorrow, but he was not being honest. You were lucky if he finished them in a month's time. He would always ask for a deposit, and once you had paid the deposit you were trapped. Every day he would say 'I will finish your shoes tomorrow', but tomorrow never seemed to come.

Just across the road lived a businessman called Abdullahi Harib, a trader in hides and skins, and by our standards he was very wealthy. I can still visualize him, a middle-aged trader who was always smartly dressed and well-mannered. Next to our hut, on the left, in front of the Abdullahi Harib and Ballase premises were meat, vegetable and milk market. On the far left of the market was the Grand Mosque where people gathered for Friday prayers. Immediately on the left of the market was the blacksmith, where knives, machetes and spears were made. Yassin Arraleh was the man who ran that business and he had two daughters, Adego and Nimo, and a son, Awil. Adego was in the same form as me in school, though I don't know her whereabouts today. Nimo was the more beautiful and well known of the two. She initially started a career in teaching but later became a singer, and she has since become a famous and much-admired artist. She now lives in the UK. I admired her looks, but did not have the courage to approach her as I was a very shy boy.

My Uncle Robleh also wanted to make plenty of money. He decided to open a corner shop in Sheikh to serve the needs of nomads coming to the town to sell their livestock – it was a convenience store, in effect. His two elder sons, Hassan and Hussein, also joined him. I remember Hassan being very tall and handsome; he seemed very cultured in his new-looking, bright-coloured shirts and khaki trousers. Hassan used to live with his maternal uncle, his mother's brother, in Hargeisa, the capital of

Somaliland, which was a long way from Sheikh. His uncle was a government officer. Hassan was well educated, especially in the Arabic language. He later joined the army.

Uncle Robleh was a bad-tempered man who was always insulting me. He often told me my brain must weigh only an ounce. I wondered how he could say such a thing, because I knew I was more intelligent than either of his sons. Perhaps deep down, he knew that, and resented it. Today in western culture we would call it emotional abuse.

He suffered from constant headaches, which he used to treat with Aspro, one of the few medicines that were available. It seemed a wonder drug at that time. He would put six tablets into a cup of hot tea, cover his head with a sheet in order to create a humid environment and swallow it quickly down. He would sweat a lot, but the headache was gone within a few minutes.

One day during the school holidays my cousin Hussein and I decided to go and see the family camels. We wanted camel's milk in order to strength our bones, as the tradition dictate. We had to hitchhike from Sheikh to the dusty town of Burao and towards the dry plains deep in the south. It took us two and half days to reach the settlement. It was the wet season and everything was green. Milk and ghee were abundant. However the place was heavily infested with mosquitoes and I was not able to sleep at night because of their biting. There were no mosquito nets or mosquito prophylaxis in the form of tablets.

We reached the settlement on the third day. When we had got there we were told that the camels were going to be moved north towards Burao, where they could eat a special type of grass called gulaan which was good for them. So again we travelled with the camels, covering hundreds of miles.

Although it was the rainy season and water and grass were available, we now came to a dry part of the country. Camels travel fast on dry ground and it is difficult to keep up with them. Somehow we managed to reach them, but we felt increasingly hungry and thirsty. Food was not such a problem, but finding water was now becoming absolutely critical.

By the time we had found a small quantity of water in an artificial pond we had nearly died of thirst. The water was discoloured and smelly, but it was enough for us to drink in order to survive.

By the seventh day we were close to Burao. After our little adventure, which had lasted a fortnight, we decided to come home without telling our cousin. We were not far from our beloved town of Sheikh.

On arrival back at Sheikh, my cousin Sayid asked me to go and see his family, who were a three-hour walk east of the town. On the way I began to feel ill. Soon I felt as weak as a kitten and could go no further. Fortunately a stranger came to the rescue. His name was Ilac and he was a one-eyed man, a cawar in Somali. He was a porter who carried heavy things for people to earn his living. Ilac was just like a gladiator.

He hoisted me on to his back and carried me for three hours until we got back to Sheikh. If he had not saved me I would certainly have died.

It turned out that I had contracted malaria from the mosquito bite while travelling to the nomadic settlement south of Burao, a big problem in Somalia as in much of Africa. Fortunately, Sheikh Hospital was now up and running. My Uncle Robleh obtained 12 malaria tablets from the hospital and gave me four at once, then two more later and the rest over the next two days. It was one of the few kind things he did for me. It did the trick and I soon recovered.

I did not get on well with my uncle, but at least his arrival in Sheikh allowed me to swap my concrete floor for a comfortable mattress. His shop had one room at the back, so we made it our sleeping quarters. This was much better than the hut, especially as it had a toilet, a simple hole with a concrete top. There was still no running water, but there was some improvement in our food supply. I started to work in the shop in the afternoons after finishing school for the day.

Another distant uncle then also opened a shop in the town. Sayid was a farmer and his wife and children lived a three-hour journey from the town, but he needed the income from the shop to supplement his earnings from the farm, which was very much at the mercy of the dry climate and was becoming more so as rain seemed to be getting more and more scarce. Uncle Sayid asked me to join him at the shop, which was an opportunity I could not afford to miss. I was expecting him to pay me something, but he never gave me any money. However I did at least have a place to stay free of charge, and free food.

We used to sell practically everything there, including sugar and flour. We had no proper bags or boxes, so the dry goods were sold in a folded sheet of paper. You folded it into a cone and tucked the edges in to keep it together, then poured the sugar or flour into it.

One day in September 1963 Uncle Robleh took me and my cousin Hussein off to the primary school to enrol. I liked the teachers and was very impressed by how professional they seemed. However they would only agree to enrol Hussein, as I was too young. I had to wait a year before I was able to join him. That was a very frustrating time as I could not wait to go to a proper school and get away from the caning, the hard work and the poverty.

When I was able to follow Hussein to the primary school in 1964 I found it a great relief. The only problem was that it was half a mile from the town and I had to walk.

The primary school was very different from the nursery. There was structure to the teaching and we had many more subjects – we learned mathematics, science and languages, including Arabic. We learned everything in English, as the official written language of Somalia, because there was no written Somali language in those days. That was when I started to get to know English.

The study material was provided by the school, including exercise books and pencils, which was a bonus as I certainly could not have paid for them. There was a playground where we played football. This was the first place I had known which was actually for play.

One of the teachers was an Arabic teacher called Oraf. His name meant 'angry man' in Somali and he was indeed often angry. He always carried a cane and would use it freely to hit any student who failed to answer a question. That man should never have been a teacher, but unfortunately beating children was part of our culture.

Another teacher, Dayib, taught mathematics, and he was even harsher than Oraf. Dayib suffered from an undiagnosed mental illness. He would function well for a year or so and then there would be a period when he was so manic that he could not work at all and had to stay at home.

Dayib had a particular way of hitting us children which was extremely painful. He knew there was a particularly tender spot on our bottoms, and he would locate it by tightening your trousers, and then hit it very hard. It was unfortunate that our culture allowed this sort of thing to happen. We hated him so much. We told each other that God had punished him for the merciless beating of innocent children by giving him an incurable mental illness.

Later when I found a book about educational psychology, I realised that those old teachers had it all wrong. I discovered that that the old idea of punishing children to make them does better is misguided. While there is a place for punishment, a reward system is the only effective way of getting the best from children. Rewarding a child increases self-esteem and confidence. I also learned that one should ask open questions, not direct ones with yes or no answers, to encourage a child to open up.

The chief of our tribe, Hajji Yassin, lived near my uncle's corner shop. He was the most powerful man in Sheikh, and famous for his intellect. He was also a very kind and helpful man. As a salaried civil servant he was not rich, but his wife, Ash Hassan, ran her own business and had become one of the richest people in the area. This was a remarkable achievement in a society where women are subordinate to men. She was very tall and fair skinned; in fact to us she seemed more white than black.

On a number of occasions Ash invited me to her house to eat, usually in the morning. Sadly for them, they had no children of their own. Hajji Yassin had been urged to father children to inherit his legacy, but although Ash bore him no children he chose not to take any more wives, as he could have done.

One of my father's two sisters lived in Burao, south of Sheikh, and during school holidays I would go and stay with her there. She had three children, two sons and a daughter. The elder son, Yassin, had a corner shop in Burao and I started to help him in the shop, which sold dates, cigarettes and camel's milk. People there preferred camels' milk to cows' milk and I too soon adopted the habit. Camels' milk is very concentrated and it is delicious when fermented and sugar is added. Legend holds that it cures diabetes.

The second son, Abdullah, a smart, flamboyant and outgoing personality, was a businessman, although his business hit trouble later on through government interference. People used to gossip about him bringing alcohol from the port of Berbera to Burao, although drinking and trading alcohol were prohibited. He was talkative and very kind, and I admired him a lot.

At the end of my four years of primary education we had to take an examination before going on to the intermediate school (the equivalent of an English primary school). There was something very odd about the way the examination was held. Some of the older fifth year students returned to the school to help us. The other students taking the exam wrote the questions they were trying to answer on scraps of paper and threw them through the windows. The year five boys would answer the questions and throw the scraps of paper back through the window for them. This went on until we finished the examination.

While this was going on the invigilator simply sat there, taking no notice. It was clear that some of the parents had assumed the examination would be difficult and were afraid their sons would fail, so they had bribed the invigilator with money and food to allow their sons to cheat. I was not sure exactly how the system was organised, but it was executed with precision. Most of the children passed, of course.

This would not be the last time I would have to deal with unfairness, dishonesty and political corruption. Life had been extremely hard, but at least it had been peaceful. I did not know that Somalia was about to enter a period of strife and conflict which would continue until the present day.

Chapter Three

POVERTY AND POLITICS

It was when I moved to the intermediate school that political troubles began to influence my life. Somalia has been torn by conflict for the past half century. Until 1960 it was a British Protectorate. In that year the north and south were united to form an independent Somali Republic, but it was not to last. The last democratic elected government in Somalia was sworn in 1969 and Mohamed Ibrahim Egal, a well-known politician from Somaliland, was elected Prime Minister. However that October the president, Abdirashid Ali Sharmarke, was shot dead by his own bodyguard on a visit to the town of Las Anod, south of Burao, and the government was toppled by a military coup. Egal was thrown in jail. Mohamed Siad Barre seized power and established the Somali Democratic Republic.

A Supreme Revolutionary Council assumed power, renaming the country the Somali Democratic Republic. Parliament was dissolved and the constitution suspended.

The revolutionary army established large-scale public works programmes and began an urban and rural literacy campaign, which helped to increase the literacy rate. The new régime's foreign policy was to strengthen Somalia's traditional and religious links with the Arab world, and it eventually joined the Arab League.

At the time the revolution was welcomed by many and it was an exciting time for Somalia, but excitement was the last thing I needed. I wanted to be allowed to get on with my education. I had a gut feeling that things were not going to be as easy as people thought. I relied heavily on my cousin's retail business, but unfortunately it was one of the first casualties of the coup, because Uncle Sayid decided to close the shop and go back to the nomadic life. He literally left me out in the cold, without food or shelter. I felt betrayed, and had nowhere to turn. My Uncle Robleh's shop also closed soon afterwards.

I continued attending school, as education was my only hope of going on to a better life. However, although the intermediate school was a boarding school offering free board and lodging for students from all over the country, this service was not available to boys from Sheikh itself, who were expected to have their own accommodation. The real reason for this was that most of the students were from areas west of Hargeisa, where the education minister himself came from, even though Mr Egal, our cousin, was the prime minister. He failed to influence the policy of education, which was unfair to us as local students. The education minister was favouring his own people at the expense of ours, which was dominant in Sheikh. It was the first time I had tasted the unfairness of the education system. There were even students from Djibouti, a French colony at that time. It was difficult to comprehend how students from Djibouti could have the right to free board and lodging while we had none.

When we finished primary school we were told that there was no classroom for us to sit in. The intermediate school was very large with numerous buildings and unoccupied classes, so I could not understand why were there no classes for the local boys.

Fortunately, one day the education minister came to Sheikh to see how his students were doing. The elders asked for an urgent meeting and threatened to stop him leaving Sheikh until our education was sorted out. He soon made sure it was done. At last we had started our education in earnest.

The intermediate school was an hour's walk away from the primary school, but that was not the biggest problem where I was concerned - I had other worries. I still had no place to sleep and nothing to eat. However I had a distant relative working at the school, a well-respected local man called Abdurrahman Jama, a teacher of religious studies. Abdurrhaman heard about my hardship and decided to help me. He persuaded the head teacher to allow me to eat in the students' mess once a day, the main meal at midday after classes finished. I was delighted, as it meant I could fill my stomach at least once a day. I was somewhat humiliated, but that didn't matter. I had to live in an unforgiving world, where only the fittest could survive.

The food in the students' mess was nothing but boiled rice with a little oil and salt. It lacked nutrients and most of the students suffered malnutrition, which caused bleeding of gum and in one case bone disease. I developed rickets, which led to bow legs. My body, by and large, was underdeveloped. Fortunately these diseases did not affect my brain, but the whole experience left me with deep psychological scars.

In fact I was lucky to get that midday meal and I was grateful to Mr Jama. Other pupils were given no food at all and had to leave school altogether.

Of course, I now had another pressing issue - finding somewhere to live. I was helped by my friend Hussein, the son of the Mayor of Sheikh. Ibrahim was a brother of Hajji Yassin, the powerful tribal leader. Before becoming Mayor he had been a successful businessman. He owned many houses and other properties both in Sheikh and the sea port of Berbera, including a one-bedroom house in the town centre. It was big enough to accommodate two single beds, so Hussein asked me to stay with him there.

I was delighted with these arrangements. The only drawback was that there was no electricity or running water (like most buildings in Sheikh) and we had to use paraffin lamps to do our homework. We had no income and most of the time we had no money to buy paraffin, though Hussein's father would often give us money for it. On many nights we had to wait for the full moon to study or do our homework.

My mother very generously gave me a hundred Somali shillings, and I decided to spend some of it on a bed. I had been sleeping on a mat ever since I had started nursery school. I bought a single bed and mattress from a trader, thinking I had got a bargain.

I did not realise that the bed had been stolen, from my own school! The next thing that happened was a visit from a police officer. He confiscated the bed and the mattress and I was locked up in a small, smelly room with some other students who had been involved in selling stolen beds. I was kept there for a week before being released without charge. So I had wasted 40 shillings and had nothing to show for it.

For school I wore short trousers, a white shirt and my goatskin shoes. On Fridays, when the school was closed, I would wash and iron my shirt and shorts in cold water, ready for the inspection which took place every Saturday. One day I decided not to bother with these tasks as usual but to go and play with my friends in a nearby valley instead. When my teacher saw my dirty clothes at the inspection he sent me home. I had to run back to the town, wash them and put them on wet before I could go back to school. Fortunately they dried in the heat on my way back to school. I did not need to iron them this time.

The coup caused considerable disruption to the education system. A new batch of teachers was brought up from the south, where the official language was Italian, so they were Italian-speaking and used an Italian-based system. Their brief was to promote the new government's socialist ideals. The head teacher, Muse Wadaad, was extremely strict. He was from the Dhulbahante tribe, the people who had assassinated our president. He seemed to be less interested in culture than smoking cigarettes and driving his car. I was pretty sure he had only just taken up smoking.

I finished intermediate school in 1970 when I was 14 years old, and moved on to the secondary school. Entrance to the secondary school was highly competitive and most of my friends were left behind, including my friend Hussein and my two cousins, Hassan and Hussein. Hassan went to join the army and Hussein left school and went to work for Mr Ballase, the shoemaker. I was not sure why he chose that job as it was rough work with poor pay and conditions. Perhaps he had become disillusioned by the bureaucratic aspects of education in Somalia and the uncertainty of finding a job once you left school.

My motives were totally different from those of the rest of my friends. I was looking much further ahead. I always believed that good education would lead me to a better life. Because I was the eldest son, people urged me to marry early and have children according to the tradition of Somalis, but I resisted that temptation. My only goal was to complete my education and get a job where I could earn a proper salary.

I started secondary school at a time of great social change. The military government adopted socialism with the aim of creating a more equal society in terms of education, health and social needs, but it was all done in too much haste, without proper thought or planning. It destroyed the fabric of Somali society, especially in the northern regions. In the south of Somalia, the education system and the economy were based on a system derived from the Italian system, whereas in the north our way of life and educational system were based on British values.

One day a group of football players and folk dancers came to Sheikh to put on a show. They were touring the northern regions as a way of promoting both the government agenda and sport in general. In the heat of the afternoon their football team played our school team, and although our team was the strongest team in the north, it was badly beaten.

The secondary school had a large and beautiful theatre, a kulmiye, and in the evening the company put on a spectacular drama production there. The drama was called Shabeel Naagood, meaning 'the tiger and the girls'. The 'tiger' was a well-known singer, Ahmed Ali Egal from the Majerten tribe, and among the girls was Marian Mursal, a famous and beautiful singer and dancer. I was amazed to see that she was wearing a tiny mini-skirt and much of her body was on show. Ahmed Egal actually embraced this woman during the performance! I had never seen such things before, and nor had many of the other people watching. I found it shocking and exciting at the same time.

Sheikh was a small town with a strong religious background, so there was little tolerance of anything that was overtly sexual. The audience were astonished by the explicit sexuality in the production, as they had never seen anything like it before. Both the dancers and the footballers were demonstrating the fundamental difference between the south and the north of Somalia, at least in cultural terms. While in the south people were tolerant and might have approved of any public representation of sex, in the north it has remained taboo to the present day.

For me, the show was inspiring and an experience I have never forgotten, but not surprisingly, the religious establishment denounced the drama in strong terms. It was just as well the company left early the next morning. In hindsight the revolution was promoting socialism, which was basically anti-religion and intolerant of religious rules and figures. From that day on, religion began to lose its iron grip on our society.

This was my first visit to Sheikh Secondary School, which was to become my residence for the following four years. I was delighted to be learning in a place where so many prominent students had studied before me; the school has produced many leading intellectuals and politicians. It had a warm and homely environment compared to what I was used to. Every day I looked forward to my studies. The equipment all came from England, so we had English desks and chairs, English stationery and English pens and pencils. Some of the teachers were English too, while others were Russian or Somalis. After the revolution took its effect most of the English teachers left, so we were left with Russian teachers who did not speak much English.

The military government were very keen to get a written form of the Somali language adopted, so in 1972 intermediate and secondary school students and teachers were ordered to go off and teach written Somali to the nomads. The schools had to be closed for a year to make this possible. This was a stupid idea which was never going to work. Nomads are on the move all the time – how can they be made to follow a course?

I was sent to stay in a small village called Go'o on the road from Burao to Hargeisa, which had only a hundred inhabitants. Here I was looked after by a local nomad family for the duration of the campaign, but they were given no money to feed us so I don't know how they managed. Go'o stood on top of a mountain overlooking a beautiful wildlife reserve where sheep and goats were excluded. There were dik-dik (a small antelope species) and a variety of other animals. I tried exploring the caves on the reserve, but we were not allowed to enter the deeper caves as there was a danger that we might disturb a lion.

In 1972, at end of the literacy campaign, the government ordered a population census. It was carried out with such incompetence and corruption that it was not worth doing. We were poorly trained and our morale was low, as we were forced to do without adequate payment. The forms consisted of numerous pages and were difficult to complete at one go. The language the forms were written in was vague to say the least. It was not census – it was a complete farce. Most people could not read or write, so we students were told to interview people to fill in the forms. Of course, most of us just made it up. We counted dead people, imaginary people, anything to get the forms completed and returned.

While the census was being carried out a severe drought began, but the government expected us to carry on collecting forms anyway. They refused to acknowledge that anything was wrong. That drought went on and on, from 1972 through to 1974, and by the time it had finished many thousands of animals had died, as well as many people. Such a drought was unprecedented in Somalia at that time. I saw people and livestock dying on a scale we had never seen before. The Russians sent some people south to resettle near Kismayo. They were always very happy to send people to another part of the country, though it could cause great suffering.

It was not until I finished primary school education in 1968 and moved to the secondary school that for the first time I discovered an interest beyond simple day-to-day survival – reading.

Sheikh Secondary School had a wonderful library with a supply of books imported from England as a gift from the British council. At the end of the school year they used to throw out books, including used or half-used exercise books and fancy HB pencils. These items used to come into my uncle's shop, so we could use the paper for bags.

We had a tradition of poetry and song, but reading was not part of the Somali culture. I found the books in the school library fascinating and derived enormous pleasure from exploring them. Most of them were in English, which we learned as a subject in its own right.

There were books about education and learning and the world around us. Some of the books were about biology, including human anatomy. I found those books very interesting, and for the first time they gave me the idea that I would like to be a doctor one day. Somalia had no native doctors then; the few doctors in the country were from overseas. Most of them were Russians.

I started to explore the books out of my own interest. There was a reference library and a lending library and I started to take out two books every week from the lending library. There were thousands of titles by famous British and American authors. I borrowed Erle Stanley Gardner's Perry Mason crime novels and was enthralled by Daniel Defoe's Robinson Crusoe, as well as Animal Farm by George Orwell, but my favourites were the crime novels of Agatha Christie. I used to very much enjoy reading those books. They painted a picture of a world which was very strange to me, in which people lived in comfort in big houses, with servants and all the food and entertainment they wanted. I was beginning to realise that there was a world outside Somalia which was very different from the one I knew.

I finished secondary school in 1976, when I was 20 years old. I now had to go into national service. This meant a year teaching elementary and intermediate schoolchildren, somewhere in Somalia. Where I was going would be decided by the authorities.

It was the beginning of a series of adventures which would take me very far from Sheikh and the life I knew.

Chapter Four

NATIONAL SERVICE

When I left Sheikh, I still did not know where I was going to be posted for my national service. With me was a good friend called Ahmed Abdi and another boy called Abdirahman Shotali. It was a big adventure for me to leaving my home region for the first time, particularly not knowing where I was going, and I was very pleased to have my friends with me, particularly Ahmed.

We had been told to go to Bosaso, a town on the coast in the north east of Somalia, which is now one of the headquarters of the infamous Somalian pirates. Once there we would be told where our final destination would be. Together we hitched a ride on an old government lorry as far as Las Anod, the town where the president of Somalia, President Sharmarke, had been assassinated in 1969. We arrived around 6 pm, and as we were afraid to trust to a hotel because of what had happened to our president, we slept in the lorry. The night passed uneventfully, and the following day we set out for the next stop, Garowe.

We reached Garowe, a dry and waterless town, late the next morning, tired and needing rest. Garowe lies in a strategic position between the north east, north west and south of Somalia and today it is another of the towns used by the Somalian pirates as a base.

Our plan was to stay the night there and set off the next day. We were not impressed by Garowe. Everywhere we went we could not escape an appalling smell; the stink of rotting corpses. We never did find out where it came from.

We looked around, but we could find nowhere to sleep. The only hotel was full. Fortunately there was a guest house near the main hotel with one room available to rent. A man had died in the room the previous night and we felt the curse of death was upon it, but we had no choice but to wait for it to be cleaned. When we were able to get into the room we found it still stank of death, but we were so tired that we slept for three hours just the same.

Early the next day, after morning prayer, we set off for Qardho, a small hill town of about 200 inhabitants between Garowe and Bosaso. It was still dark when we left. The road was extremely rough and our old lorry struggled to negotiate the many twists and turns. We had left before breakfast was served, so we were soon very hungry.

At midday we came to a tiny village where we managed to find some dates and frozen milk - we never worked out how there could be frozen milk in a village without electricity. Ahmed refused to drink the milk, but the rest of us were so hungry that we took the risk. Fortunately it tasted good and there were no ill effects.

At sunset we finally reached Qardho, where we had a strange welcome from the local children, who showered us with stones. Fortunately we escaped serious injury. At this point we parted company with our lorry and its driver.

In the morning we were hoping for a traditional Somali

breakfast of pancakes or bread with tea, but instead they were serving spaghetti, tea and meat. It was very strange to eat meat at seven in the morning. 'They must think we are hyenas!' said Shotali. 'Only hyenas or foxes eat meat in the morning.'

We tried to find another restaurant, but there was nothing else. We were now very hungry, so we decided to eat the spaghetti and meat.

The following day we met up with some other teachers from the Somalian capital, Mogadishu in the south, and they invited us to ride in their lorry with them. It was in much better condition than ours had been. They were Italian speakers, which caused some confusion. As we rode in the lorry they kept saying 'scusa', which of course meant 'excuse me', but we didn't know that at the time. We thought it was the Somali word 'skoos', meaning squeeze, so every time they said it we tried to squeeze in more tightly. Finally Abdirahman Shotali complained about being constantly asked to 'skoos' and we northerners all laughed, but the Italian Somalis did not get the joke at all.

The next morning we headed down from the hills for Bosaso. At sunset we stopped at an outpost called Karin Bosaso, where we ate goats' meat and pasta in a nomad restaurant. They were selling two types of goats' meat – fresh meat from animals which had been slaughtered that day and meat seasoned with spices and pepper from the previous day, which was not very fresh but cheaper. Without electricity there were no fridges, and meat lasted only a very short time in that heat before it went bad.

Bosaso is a major port and the capital city of the Puntland region, which has an ancient history. It is thought to be the area described by the ancient Egyptians as the Land of Punt, from which thousands of years ago they imported gold, aromatic resins, exotic wood, ivory and valuable animals, as well as slaves.

We reached Bosaso about eight o'clock at night and found a small hotel where we spent the next two nights. While we were there we met up with the Director of Education for the region. His name was Dhega Weyn, which means 'the man with the big ears'. His ears were indeed very big, although he was a small man. Somalis are not afraid of giving people names depending on the way they look, and no one takes offence.

I wanted to be paired with my friends Ahmed and Abdirahman, as I would be in a region where the culture and the weather were very different from home. We felt we were in a strange land and would need each other's company. However, Dhega Weyn had other ideas. He said he was going to post us separately, to places where we could afford to eat on our meagre salaries. He was sending Ahmed to a small village called Hurdia, on the Indian Ocean coast south of the Horn of Africa, while I would be going to Aluula. Abdirahman was sent to another town south of Hurdia, called Iskushuban, on the Indian Ocean.

Aluula is a small coastal town in the extreme north east of Somalia, almost on the point of the Horn of Africa. The actual Horn is marked by Cape Guardafui, about 30 miles to the west. The town is cut off from the interior by steep mountains, so it is impossible to reach it by road unless you have a well-equipped four-wheel drive, preferably a new Land Rover, and even then it would be a long and difficult journey. I was going to have to fly there, quite an adventure for a young man who had never seen the sea or travelled in anything more sophisticated than a truck.

With two other young teachers from Bosaso, I boarded an old and battered-looking DC3 for the flight from Bosaso airport to Aluula. I was a little scared, but I was very excited. The runway was very rough and the take-off was hair-raising, but the flight went without incident and we were soon in Aluula.

Aluula is a small and very isolated town with just a junior school, a hospital and a municipal office. There was only one sandy street. Its principal industry is fishing, and most of the locals work in one of the two fish storage and processing factories. It is a historic town with a long history of links with the outside world, thanks to its position on the Horn of Africa.

I was alarmed to discover when I arrived that the principal diet for people in Aluula was fish. Aluula was full of the smell of fish. I had never even seen a fish before, let alone eaten one, so I was worried that I would not like it. Although Sheikh is only 40 miles from the coast, without efficient transport and refrigeration it was still too far to transport fresh fish.

On the first night an accountant took us to eat in a restaurant in the town which served bread rolls with pieces of fried fresh fish. I told him that I couldn't eat fish because of the small bones, which would stick in my throat and kill me. They laughed out loud at this, as they were all used to eat fresh fish and knew that I was exaggerating the problem, but I was only repeating what I had heard. I tried the fish and it was very nice, but it took me 20 minutes to eat it because I had to check every flake for bones. The others thought it was very funny.

When I got used to fish I would go and eat it every day, as soon as I smelled it frying. From that day onwards it became my favourite food. They also served dried whale meat, which they sold to Mogadishu. The dried whale meat looked like sticks and had a strange smell. Somalis used it to make a rich sauce for pasta which was popular in the south of Somalia.

Aluula was very dependent on fish. At one point, in the hot summer when the sea was rough, we ran out of supplies and had nothing left to eat but flour. The restaurants ran out of food before we had finished classes. The mayor had to give more money to the restaurants so that they could still provide food for us while we were busy teaching in school.

I arrived in Aluula at the peak of the revolution, when Mohamed Siad Barre had just set up the Somali Revolutionary Socialist Party. Everyone was enjoying the euphoria of having a new régime, but like most revolutions, it was by no means all good news. There was no tolerance of alternative views or membership of the wrong tribe. Twenty businessmen in the town had been arrested on trumped-up charges of fraud and their trial was about to finish as I arrived in Aluula. General Geelle, Siad Barre's hangman, was the judge and although he was from the same tribe, they had no chance of justice. They were accused of exporting frankincense to the Gulf States, where it was used to perfume homes, without paying tax. They were all given long prison sentences. There was no prison in Aluula, so they were simply kept in a house. There was nowhere for them to run to, as Aluula was a landlocked town, so iron bars were unnecessary. If they had escaped from the prison and gone on the run they would soon have died from lack of food and water.

Our lodgings were next to the school and we slept in two rooms behind the classes. A local girl was our cook and cleaner. One night we found her having some sort of nervous breakdown. It seemed she had been possessed by the Jinn, an evil spirit. She screamed and took her headscarf off and exposed her long and beautiful hair. She threw herself on the floor.

One of my friends, who seemed well versed in the Muslim religion, asked us to read a passage from the Koran to her. We tried that, but it had no effect. The girl continued to scream and tear her hair, and was spitting saliva everywhere.

In Somalia there are healers who have special powers to treat people afflicted by the Jinn. Two such healers, one tall and one short, were called to help us. They both lived in houses nearby. They appeared very strange; in fact to me they looked as if they were from another planet. They had very dark skin and were strangely dressed.

We told them what had happened, and the shorter man immediately recognised the symptoms. He clearly knew what he was doing. The healer asked for a type of frankincense, called foox. He burned this in a stove and put it near her nose. Then he started twisting her left little finger very hard and ordered the spirit to leave. She screamed more and told him to stop. Then he commanded the Jinn to go out of her.

This somewhat harsh treatment continued for about 30 minutes. The woman must have been feeling a lot of pain,

Mohamud with Ibrahim Suleiman in a studio photo taken in Burao, 1974

With friends in Hargeisa, 1986 – Mohamed Adino,
ME, Essa Nur, Farhan Liban

With Mohamud Adino, Hargeisa 1986

Hargeisa, 1987, with a group of Somali doctors from Mogadishu

Soon after my arrival in Rome in 1988 with Said Saleh,
Ahmed Abdirahman and Ahmed Hashi

In the Palazzo Venezia, Rome, 1989

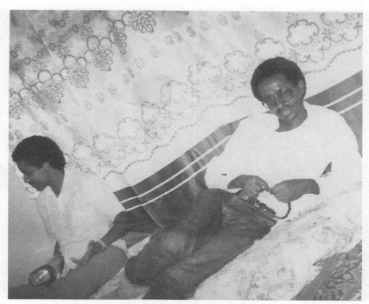

with my best friend Ahmed Abdi

1989 – in the Istituto d'Ematologia, Rome with a visiting Chinese doctor

About to depart Rome Airport for London, December 1992

Rome Airport – the departure of Dr Abdillahi Essa (seated with ME) to Canada. Standing are Dr Haid, Dr Hussein Hanfi, Dr Mohamed Abdirahman and another colleague (name unknown).

With friends at the Istituto d'Ematologia, 1992

In the Piazza Fontana with Ahmed Abdirahman

The day of my engagement to Ubah in 1991,
with Mohamud Ibrahim and Ali Ismael

With Ubah's uncle, Ahmed Abdirahman - Ubah is to the right

Ahmed Abdirahman trying to undo the xeedho at my wedding

My family at Bristol Zoo, 2010

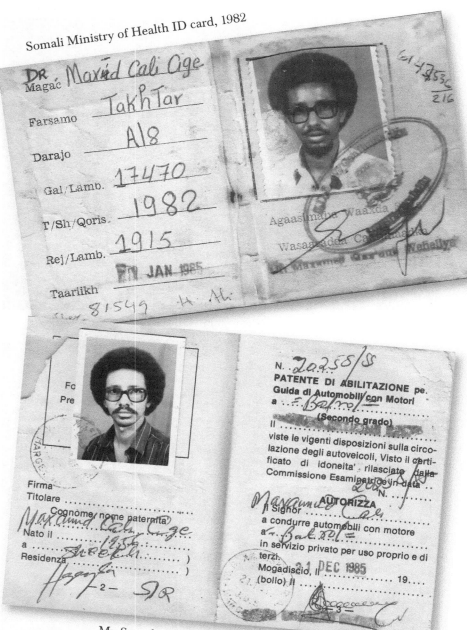

Somali Ministry of Health ID card, 1982

My Somali driving licence, 1985

Somali ID card 1987

Magaca	MAXAMUUD
Aabbaha	CALI
Awowga	CIGE
Naaynaas	NIL
Hooyada	MUUMINA ABOKOR
Ku dhashay	SHEEKH
Sanadka	1956
Jinsiyada	SOMALI
Shaqada	DOCTOR
Xaas ahaan	NIL
Deggan	HARGEISA
Waddada	26/JUUN
W. G. ee Q.	36058/87
Joogga	1.70
Oogada	CAADI
Indhaha	GAWD — Timaha — MADOW
Astaan Gaar	NIL

Student card, Rome 1991

Italian ID card, 1992

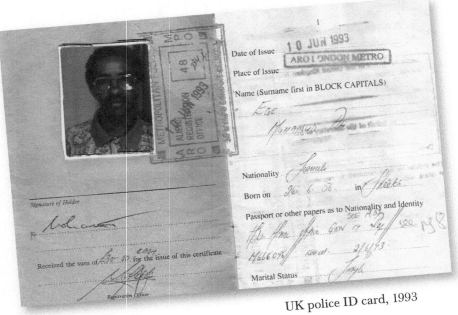

UK police ID card, 1993

UK police identity card, 1994

particularly from her little finger, but in the end the treatment worked for her. He was a good healer and she soon came round. I found that a remarkable experience, and perhaps it was one of the events that later gave me an interest in mental illness.

I read as much as I could in Aluula. It was here that I read my last Agatha Christie novel, The Big Four, which was different from the others because it consisted of four stories about four great fictional detectives from different countries.

I also found and read a psychology book which dealt with issues of child education and child psychology. The latter impressed me very much and I applied some of its ideas to my students, such as rewarding a child rather punishing him, and asking children open questions rather than closed questions, which encourages them to respond more freely.

Despite the lack of facilities in Aluula, I was well fed and life was good. We would go swimming every day and we soon got to know the local girls. One of my fellow teachers had sex with one of the girls and with her mother as well, which the rest of us found shocking. He was proud of his achievement, but I found it very strange as my upbringing was totally different from his. For us it was forbidden to make sexual advances to girls before marriage, let alone go to bed with your girlfriend's mother. In hindsight, this was one of the areas where the cultures of the north and south of Somalia differ. I found it a tasteless episode.

The salary of the teachers was very low in general, but our pay was even less as we were not fully-fledged teachers. Even so I was able to save some money as there was nothing in Aluula to spend it on, and by the time I left I had managed to save 600 Somali shillings from my salary, because there was nothing to spend the money on. There were no big shops and no cinemas. We were unable even to find a barber, so my hair grew enormous - like the Afro-American styles of the 1970s - and I had to use a big wooden comb (they were specially made locally) until I came back to Burao.

I finished my teaching in Aluula in June 1977, just as the hot season was about to start. Now it was time for the homeward journey to Sheikh. This time I decided to go by sea back to Bosaso instead of by air, and I managed to hitch a lift on a big privately-owned boat which was heading for Yemen. It is much easier to get a lift in African countries than it is in the west, as people believe that by helping people they are saving up credit for the afterlife.

Just as my flight to Aluula had been a first, this was the first time I had been on board a boat. I was looking forward to it, but unfortunately it was an extremely rough trip.

I knew we were in trouble as soon as we reached the open sea. The sea was very deep here and the winds built the waves up to huge heights. Soon they looked more like mountains than waves and were washing over the entire boat. The whole world seemed to be going round, and everyone became nauseous. I was very sick and started vomiting. I was so ill that I could not keep any food or fluids down and dehydration began to set in. It was not until midnight that I managed to swallow a few sips of water. We arrived in Bosaso early in the morning and were very relieved to be able to spend time recovering in the heat.

Two days later I arranged a lift with someone who was going to

Burao in his Land Rover. We headed inland and up into the mountains, bound for the town of Erigavo before continuing our journey to Burao. The road was very rough and we were soon bruised black and blue from bouncing around in the back.

At night the temperature in the hills soon dropped almost to freezing, and I had only a shirt on and a thin sheet for protection. The cold was terrible, especially after so long in the heat of Aluula. When we got to Erigavo I sat in the sun for two hours when we got there, to warm up. I had a nice breakfast with hot food in a local restaurant. I felt better after the trouble in the night, but there was no time to waste as I had to set off to Burao the same day.

The journey was difficult as we had to negotiate Saraar, a vast expanse of waste land between Erigavo in the high mountains and Burao down on the plains. The road was very rough, as we knew it would be, and there was a terrible red dust which penetrated into all our belongings. I had a small bag in which I kept my two extra shirts. The colour of the shirts changed from clean white into a bright red, which refused to go away even after repeated washing. In the end the shirts had to be thrown into the dustbin.

I stayed in Burao for a couple of days before setting off to my beloved home town of Sheikh. Finally, after another ride in a lorry which carried livestock to the sea port of Berbera for exporting to the Gulf States, I arrived in Sheikh.

It was strange to be back in the town I knew after so long away. I realised that I had hardly missed my family and didn't feel the need to go and see them. That's how things are in the Somali culture – no one says 'I've missed you' or 'you never come to see me'. Nice words like 'please' and 'thank you' are not part of our culture. Someone would have passed the news to my mother that I had come back, but she didn't know or care too much where I had been as long as I was still alive and kicking, and would not expect me to go and see her. Neither would my brother and sisters.

Things were different in Sheikh now, because we were at war with Ethiopia, our neighbour. It was a devastating war for both countries. Many young men and women lost their lives.

After a month back in Sheikh I had to go to Mogadishu, the capital, for the second part of my national service. This was not a matter of choice – I had no option. Here we were to be given military training so that we could defend our country in case of war. There was a military camp near the airport, south of Mogadishu, called Hallane, from a Somali word meaning to clean. It housed a military training facility for secondary school leavers.

The road between Burao and Mogadishu had been built by the Chinese and it was still under construction when I started the first part of the national service. It had however been completed by the time I came back to Sheikh. It made travel to the south relatively easy, but it still took three days to travel to Mogadishu in a modern bus.

Going south was another very new experience for me. Southern Somalia is a paradise compared with the north, because it is low-lying land with far more rainfall. As you approach Mogadishu the land turns green and you see cool, fast-flowing rivers. The fields had cattle grazing, which we never had in the north. Unfortunately, Somalis from the north have no time for cows or their milk – they prefer camels' milk. There was fruit, even bananas, the first ones I had ever seen. The whole experience down there was very different. People were speaking a different language, a mixture of Somali with Italian, and in a very strange dialect.

Life at Hallane was hard, though I was pleased to be with Ahmed Abdi again. The training was rigorous and very demanding and the discipline was strict. Ahmed liked the PE but I did not enjoy it at all. We went for long marches and learned to handle guns, including Russian Kalashnikovs. We learned how to assemble the guns and take them apart and how to operate and clean them, but we were not allowed to practise with live ammunition, so I don't know how effective we would have been if we had had to fight!

Our sleeping quarters were bunk beds in big houses, each of which housed 200 trainees. We were up every morning at five for two hours of running and PE, and then we would have what they called breakfast, which was nothing but a cup of black tea and a piece of bread sprinkled with sesame oil.

After breakfast we would go for military training and drill until 1 pm, when we would have a one-hour lunch break. In contrast to our meagre breakfast, lunch was enormous. A big plate would be piled high with spaghetti and oil. Those of us who were from the north found we could not finish it because it was so big, and our stomachs were small because of our subsistence diet. The people from the south could eat it without difficulty as they were used to bigger meals.

In the evening we had another big dish of food made from a local bean with sesame oil, called diger. By the time we finished at Hallane we got used to the quantities and could eat the plates of food with no problem.

After the evening meal we would sit down together and watch a film. This was a new experience for me, as I had never seen films or television. It was very simple entertainment. There was a children's cartoon which we used to enjoy, featuring animals, including a cow and a rabbit. The rabbit talked to the cow as it appeared to be hungry, and we interpreted the mooing of the cow as saying 'bal caws ee keen', which means 'bring me some grass'. We did not understand the language, which must have been Italian. We saw Indian films too, but they were very long and it got too hot sitting there watching them, so we would not watch them all the way through.

In Somalia Friday is a rest day, like a weekend, so those trainees who had families locally would go and see their parents. They would often bring back big locked boxes of food which they kept to themselves. Those of us who were from the north had no such privileges.

The next step was enrolment for military service, which we all wanted to avoid if we possibly could. They knew nobody would join of their own accord, so they forced some of us to enrol by choosing 'volunteers' from a long queue. The chosen ones would receive more specialist instruction at a military academy on the outskirts of the capital, and then later on they would be sent to Russia to complete their training.

Unfortunately I was one of those who were chosen to go to the military academy. I hated it. I had been there for a month when another student, Ibrahim Macalesh, and I decided to escape. We were not caught, but there was an unwritten rule that trainees who escaped from the military academy had to be readmitted to Hallane and the next day, with nowhere else to go, we turned ourselves back in.

They were not too hard on us, as they understood that we had never asked to become soldiers. They told us we had to go back to the academy and bring a letter from someone in authority who knew us, saying we did not want to be part of the military. Fortunately Ibrahim knew someone who was a senior officer, and he agreed to give us a letter, which we presented at Hallane.

Abdi Yassin, Yassin Yare's second son was working in Mogadishu at this time for the fishing industry. My relative Abdullahi had a son called Omar. Today he lives and works in Birmingham, but at the time he was working in Mogadishu as an accountant.

Muse Ali, who had once lived with me in Sheikh, was also there in Hallane. One day Muse and I decided to go and see Omar and Abdi to ask for some money, or shaxaad in Somali. We knew they would have had their salaries, and it was quite usual in our society to ask a relative for money. We decided to ask for forty shillings.

Unfortunately they offered us only pocket money instead and gave us twenty shillings. But even that money was soon lost. On the streets of Mogadishu there were cardsharps, tricksters who would invite you to join their game, working in a sort of a gang. My mind was fixed on getting my hands on another 20 shillings so that each of us could have twenty. When I saw these people playing cards and winning money, I thought it would be easy to win another 20 shillings, so without thinking about the consequences I put in my 20 shillings. Of course I lost it immediately.

Suddenly we were having a very bad day. We were tired and hungry, and now we were penniless as well. We must have walked for three or four hours before we found someone, a member of our extended family, who could gave us money. He gave us five shillings to pay for a little food and transport back to Hallane.

We got back to Hallane at eleven o'clock. It was 21 October, the birthday of our beloved revolution. We were expected to celebrate the successes of the revolution, even though there were really no successes at all as the war with Ethiopia had destroyed entire communities and wrecked the economy.

A military parade was usually held on the 21st of October every year, and many dignitaries participated, including the president and his entourage. We had to take part in it. We were taken to the street where the parade was happening at 5 o'clock in the morning without having had a wink of sleep. The parade finished at midday and we were back in Hallane at two in the evening. Because of lack of sleep and tiredness we practically collapsed, and we did not wake up until the following day.

While we were at Hallane we sat for the entrance exams for the National University, the only university in Somalia. I was naturally very keen to get a place in medicine. The university had been established and run by Italians, with the help of funding from the European Economic Community (EEC). It had been set up in the early years of the revolution and was a very young university by any standards. It had various faculties, including of course a medical faculty.

In September 1978 we reported to the reception area of the registrar's office to find out which of us had got a place. The names were put on a board outside the reception area of the university. We went to see the results and I was horrified to see that my name was not on the board, as I thought I had done well. All my friends found their names on the list.

I hardly slept that night as I was fearful of being left out. We went back the next day to see the registrar and found that there had been a Mohamed Ege in the queue – his name was one letter different from mine. When they had read out my name he had thought they were calling him, so he responded. But the place had been for me.

I saw Mohamed Ege again in 1987 while attending a haematology conference in Lagos, Nigeria. He was now an employee of the Somali embassy in Nigeria. It was nice to meet him again.

In my early days at university something very unpleasant happened to me. We Muslims are prohibited from eating or drinking certain things, including alcohol. However, when you are young you sometimes go astray without thinking of the consequences. Because we are human we make mistakes, and I made a grave mistake, although I asked God for forgiveness. I am just hoping that God has accepted my prayer for forgiveness.

One night, while in Mogadishu, I went to the city centre with two of my friends and they took me to a pub. It was unusual for me to go to such places, and this was my first and my last time. I soon felt sick with the strong smell of the alcohol, but I stayed anyway. They ordered a bottle of dry gin, which was very strong. We shared the bottle and when we had finished it, they ordered three bottles of beer. I felt sick before I even started to taste the beer. Nausea overcame me and I ran out of the pub.

The whole world was spinning around me. I felt dizzy and began to vomit. I was semiconscious for about two hours, and when I came round I could hardly stand up. I had no money for a taxi, so I decided to walk back to the university campus, and got there about half past three in the morning. I felt sick, exhausted and dehydrated.

I managed to catch a few hours' sleep before attending to my morning lessons. Although I attended, my mind was not there. My body continue to ache till the following day. My friends became concerned about my state of health as they thought I was seriously ill.

Fortunately I survived the incident with no further harm, but I have never gone near a pub again since that day. Nowadays, whenever I smell alcohol, the experience comes back to me and I feel nauseous, a reaction which may stay with me for the rest of my life. I am glad that I have developed this reaction as I hope I am all the healthier for not drinking alcohol.

I was told to go to the medical faculty and we started the next day, but before we could start learning medicine we had to do a six-month crash course in the Italian language. Because the university had been set up by the Italians, all the teaching was in

Italian. This was naturally a huge obstacle. Those of us from the north, who were used to English and had never spoken Italian, found it a hopeless challenge. Many of the students gave up and left the university within a very short time. Of 100 students who began the course, half failed their end-of-year exams and left at the end of the first year. At the end of the four years, fewer than 30 of the students passed their exams and went on to become doctors.

The student accommodation and food were free of charge. The tuition was also free, and we were given 30 shillings' pocket money a month, again thanks to EEC funding. It was not a fortune, but it was good money and enough to pay for us to eat in town quite regularly.

Before I finished university in 1982 I met a doctor called Osman Adam, the Professor of Haematology. Osman was the son of the first president of the Somali Republic, Adan Cade, and he was running a blood transfusion service. Haematology was my favourite subject and I was good at it. He was trying to modernise Somalia's blood transfusion service and he had secured some funding from the Finish Government. He asked if I would consider haematology as a career, and I agreed. I joined his team later on.

I successfully finished my medicine course in 1982 and went to do a year of internship, equivalent to a foundation year in England, to consolidate what I had learned and put my theoretical knowledge into practice before practising medicine on my own. It is always good to do an extra mile in medicine and to learn more, particularly as you are dealing with people.

But I had now been away from home now for seven years, and I was beginning to feel very homesick.

Chapter Five

BACK TO THE NORTH

I had now had enough of Mogadishu and the south. In 1985 I decided to go back to Somaliland, because I had been there only once since 1978 and wanted to see my home again.

I asked for a transfer to the port of Berbera, a city dear to my heart. It is the largest sea port in Somalia and has the largest airport; both were built by the Russians during the Cold War and later enlarged by the US Government. It is the backbone of our economy.

I arrived in Berbera on May 15 1985 to work in the hospital there. It is an old general hospital, built by the British in 1918, and it had a very basic psychiatric ward among other general wards. In the psychiatric ward, the conditions were medieval - people were chained up. In fact people did not consider the psychiatric ward as a hospital but as a prison for mad people.

There was an old and outdated electroconvulsive machine which was applied to everybody with mental illness indiscriminately. The only psychiatric medication available then was Chlorpromazine.

I worked in Berbera until the following year, 1986. Because it was a big international port, built by the Russians and then developed by the Americans, there were people of all backgrounds there and it offered many opportunities to make money. I used to work for the government in the morning and run my own private clinic in the afternoon. It was very much like being a GP, as I used to treat practically everything – infections, minor injuries, tuberculosis, infectious diseases, whatever people had wrong with them. Only if people needed an operation would they be sent to Hargeisa. I was able to charge for my services and make good money, so I did very well out of it financially.

I went back to Sheikh only twice while I was working in Berbera. I was very frustrated by the narrow outlook of the people in Sheikh. I said to my friends, 'Why don't you come to Berbera and make some money?' All they would say was 'No, we can't go to Berbera, it is too hot!'

But now the climate in Sheikh had changed. When I was very young we used to have continuous rain and hail in the town, so much so that my schoolbooks would often be wet. It was very green most of the time. But now we had started to have more and longer droughts, and life was getting even harder for the nomads. The rain dried up around the time the Russians came, though I suppose we cannot really blame them for that as well as everything else! It's strange how there always seems to be a drought when there's a war. Somalians say war and drought go hand in hand. Maybe war and floods go hand in hand as well.

Since the war between Ethiopia and Somalia had ended in 1978, resistance movements had become emboldened, and they were waging civil war against the government. Extra-judicial killings, rape and lootings perpetrated by the military forces were a daily occurrence in the north. But the government forces were now encountering a force comparable to to their own. The government's hold on the country was becoming increasingly weak and resistance movements were springing up, encouraged by our old enemy Ethiopia.

There is a long history of hostility between Ethiopia and Somalia. Some Somalis claim that part of our country, the reserve area, was given to Ethiopia by the British before we became independent, and ever since then we have been trying to get it back. The Somali National Movement was running a guerrilla warfare campaign, which was highly organised, and they were having many successes against the soldiers of the military government, who were not highly motivated. Around September to October 1985 the resistance movement infiltrated the whole northern party of Somalia through a surprise attack.

One day a military unit came to Sheikh from a garrison based at Adadley near Hargeisa. Their aim was to suppress the movement by killing everyone who was sympathetic to them. They terrorized the inhabitants of the coastal villages along the road which connects the port of Berbera and Sheikh. They would have slaughtered many innocent people, but fortunately they were ambushed by the guerrillas in a winding pass on the way up Sheikh. The rebels blocked the road with one of their vehicles, surrounded them on all sides and fired on them. Most of them were killed.

The leader of the government forces was a man called Colonel Jihad, who was well known for his brutality. He was a very arrogant person, so we were happy when he was killed by the resistance movement. I was certain that he would have killed many people if he had succeeded. I actually treated some of the injured at Berbera General Hospital. Few survived from this assault.

I still wanted to be a haematologist and I had promised to join Osman, so after a year in Berbera he asked the Minister of Health to transfer me to Hargeisa, the capital of Somaliland, to manage a small and very basic blood transfusion centre. I moved there in October 1986. My work involved screening for syphilis and hepatitis, and later on the service started screening for AIDS. A group from Finland was treating TB and I worked alongside them too, so I was working in both TB and haematology. The screening work was more satisfying, although for many diseases we could not offer treatment, only diagnosis.

One day in 1986 a friend and I were driving through Hargeisa when we saw two attractive girls walking along the side of the road. We stopped to ask them if they wanted a lift, and they accepted. They were going to collect a wedding video from a house on the south side of the city. We took them to the house and then waited and brought them back. One of them was called Ubah and she was tall, slim and very good looking. I asked her out and we dated a few times. She was very young and had only just finished at secondary school. I went to her home and met her brothers and sisters, but I was not ready to get married even if she had been old enough. I certainly didn't want to return to the nomadic life I had left behind.

In 1987 I went to Lagos in Nigeria for a haematology conference. It was the first time I had travelled abroad. But when

I got back, my friend Ahmed and I were told we were being expelled from Hargeisa and forced to go back to Mogadishu.

The only reason for this was that we were from the north and therefore were considered unfit to work for our own people. The Medical Director was from the south and was hostile to the resistance, or to anyone who was thought to have links with them. We had no connection with the resistance, but they suspected we might because most of the doctors were from the opposing tribe.

Accordingly I lost my position as a director of an established service. In hindsight it was just as well this happened when it did, because in March 1988 the government was overrun by the forces of the Somali National Movement. The government collapsed in a matter of hours and there followed a massacre on a terrible scale. The rebels captured Burao and Hargeisa. It was good that Siad Barre was defeated, but around 50,000 people from the north lost their lives. They were bombarding Hargeisa and killing civilians. It was practically a civil war between government forces and the rebels.

The Russians had arrived in 1969. They had been supporting Siad Barre, but they now wanted to side with Ethiopia because it was a bigger country with a population of 60 million people, so it was considered a more valuable ally. I did not enjoy going back to Mogadishu, because it had changed completely and to me it had become a different place. Furthermore I lost my base, my friends and the connections I had made while in Hargeisa.

In Mogadishu I worked in a modern haematology centre which was responsible for the supply of a safe and adequate supply of blood to patients. The city had the largest haematology service in the country. While I was there I applied for a scholarship to go to Rome to study haematology, as I knew I would need a specialist subject to build a career.

In early August 1988, Osman went on a visit to Italy. Although I was only fourth in command I was asked to act as director during his absence, as he and his deputy were both away and so was the senior doctor. I found myself in a difficult position, as Somalis do not share the altruistic feelings of westerners about giving blood, so supplies were very limited. There was a heavy demand for blood, because it was needed in Hargeisa for the use of the army who were fighting the rebels in the north.

With so few people to give blood, the demand on our service was outstripping the supply. When the government saw that we were not supplying as much blood as they wanted, they suspected me of blocking supplies because I wanted to help the rebels. In fact this was nonsense – there simply wasn't enough blood.

One morning as I was busy taking blood from donors, two policemen in civilian clothes from the NSS, the dreaded National Secret Service, arrived and took me off to a prison in the city. Most of those who worked for the NSS were from the Marehan tribe, the tribe of the late president. They were famous for torture, rape and extra-judicial killing, so I was very scared.

I was taken to an old army camp and put in a cell. There were eleven people in each cell. We were not beaten or abused, but the conditions were dreadfully cramped; there was only one toilet and the food was appalling. I had no idea what would happen to me. I now feared for my professional future and for my life.

Most of the other inmates were army officers from Somaliland who were working in the north but had been brought to the capital to prevent them joining or helping the guerrilla movement. Some were high-ranking military officers. There were other prisoners who were workers for the government whose only crime was being from the north.

They kept me in that cell for a month without making any attempt to charge me. I was finally released when my director returned from Italy and protested about my incarceration. He said it was quite wrong that I was being kept prisoner when there was no evidence that I had done anything wrong, and I was doing such a valuable job for the country.

The war had now spread to Mogadishu and dreadful things were happening, often involving ordinary people who had nothing to do with the war. One night 47 people, all respectable civilians, were dragged from their homes by Government forces, taken to Mogadishu Beach and shot dead. One of those who died was a friend of mine called Yusuf, who had done his thesis in haematology. He had just finish medicine. It was a terrible atrocity. Later Amnesty International named them all in a book.

I no longer felt safe in Somalia and had become convinced that my future lay overseas. It was time to start planning a new life in Europe.

Chapter Six

FAREWELL TO SOMALIA

When I came out of that prison in Mogadishu, there was good news at last - I found my scholarship waiting for me. I was told to take my papers to the Italian Embassy, which I did. I then went to the passport office. There was another doctor who was working for the NSS. They couldn't believe that as a northerner I had never had a passport, but they quickly issued me with one. They thought everyone from the north, with the war going on, must have a passport and want to leave the country, so this was a surprise to them. They thought at first that I was a nationalist.

In October 21 1988 I left Mogadishu on a Somali Airbus to fly to Italy. The flight left around midnight. But there was a problem. It was a brand-new plane and this was its first service flight. When we flew into Yemeni airspace, the authorities did not recognise the new aircraft and ordered the pilot to return to Mogadishu or land in Yemen. He chose the former.

When I was told we had to fly back to the inferno I had just been so relieved to escape from, I was horrified. It was a terrible shock. I was even afraid that they would take me back to that dreadful prison, but fortunately, I had nothing to fear. When we landed back in Mogadishu we were taken to the departure lounge and given food and cups of tea as well as coffee. The following day they prepared an old Boeing 707 for us, a plane they knew the Yemenis would recognise.

We boarded the 707 to take off for Italy at 5 pm the next day and arrived in Rome just after midnight. It was 21 October 1988. I should have felt relieved at being safe from all the fighting and bloodshed, so it was a great relief to escape as I did, but I was still feeling very stressed and worried after all the trauma I had been through and the terrible events that had taken place in my homeland.

Many of my friends and relatives had been killed or injured for no reason. Some of them were slaughtered like animals. One poor group of Somalilanders who had been deported from Saudi Arabia at the height of the civil war were butchered with knives in cold blood at Berbera airport by the government forces. I could not put these events out of my mind and was very disturbed.

I knew I needed a specialty to progress in medicine and naturally I chose haematology. In October 1988 I enrolled in a postgraduate course at Rome University, La Sapienza. This was a highly prestigious centre run by Professor Franco Mandelli, a formidable man and a prominent authority in the field; he had been responsible for setting up the centre and under his leadership it had grown from one small ward to become a large and prestigious centre.

Professor Mandelli had been a professor since 1962 and had been running the centre at La Sapienza since 1965. He was also President of the GIMEMA Foundation (an Italian cooperative group for the treatment of adult haematological diseases),

President of the Italian National Association Against Leukaemias, Lymphoma and Myeloma. During his distinguished career he has been awarded several national and international prizes and he has received two medals from the Italian President, the Cavaliere di Gran Croce and a gold medal for achievements in the field of public health. He is an exceptional man.

I found hospital lodgings at Rome University Hospital with other Somali doctors and soon settled in. I soon took to life in Italy and to my new life as a European medical student. The teaching was excellent. I worked on the wards in the mornings and then attended lectures in the afternoons. The centre cared for patients with leukaemia and lymphoma and there were separate child and adult wards for leukaemia patients and a bone marrow transplantation ward. We also had a haematology laboratory, a histology lab and a microbiology lab, so everything we needed was there on hand. There was an out-patient clinic and a small emergency area, and in a separate building we had a blood transfusion centre. Patients receiving treatment for leukaemia were very vulnerable to illness, because the chemotherapy kills the white blood cells which normally protect you from infection.

One Friday evening a few months after I had arrived in Rome, I got home feeling very ill. I was struck down with vomiting and diarrhoea and had a sharp pain down my side. The next day, Saturday, I pressed and released the area and the pain was heightened, which told me I had the symptoms of appendicitis.

I was on my own that weekend. I walked straight into the casualty department and told them I had appendicitis. They were very sceptical, but I explained that I was a doctor and knew what was wrong with me. They admitted me quickly and I was in the operating theatre within an hour.

A few days later I tried to return to work, but Professor Amadori, the consultant I was working with, was very surprised when he saw me and sent me home to recover properly. I had to take two weeks off while I was recovering from the operation.

I spent four happy and fulfilling years working at La Sapienza. In Italy, the emphasis was very much on theoretical learning, and some trainee doctors attended only theoretical classes and did not do ward rounds. There was a lack of training in practical skills unless one was well connected. I found later that this was very unlike the UK, where it is the other way round - you get excellent skills training here but many doctors are weak on theory. In Italian universities it is actually possible to study for four years without doing any operations, especially if you are from overseas. My experience was however different, as I did both practical and theoretical skills while studying haematology.

I liked Rome very much and enjoyed the food and the climate. I did not travel much outside the city, though I did visit Bologna, another historic and beautiful city. Rome was not a cheap place to live and we had to dress quite smartly for our work, so there wasn't much money left over.

I regularly sent money to my family in Somalia – that is expected in our culture and I had no objection to this. I would get calls from my brother or sisters to send money, though your mother is always your first priority. I have never minded responding to requests for money like this, but it is better not to start sending money on a regular basis because then people may become dependent on you. I did not make a lot of money in Rome, but I had about £5000 saved up by the time I finished there.

I found people in Rome very easy to get on with and I made many friends. However they do not have the social systems of the UK and there are no large minority communities. People from other races are usually marginalised in Italy; you see many Senegalese people there earning money for their families, and there are Nigerian prostitutes working on the main through-routes in some parts of the country. In some ways Italy is like a third-world country – they don't believe in paying taxes – but they are wealthy because they don't have to import food. There is a great deal of corruption, particularly when it comes to paying taxes. Traders avoid giving you a receipt because they don't want to declare their real earnings. But people have a friendly, positive attitude to life and they are a colourful and romantic people.

While I was in Rome I would write to my brother Muse and sometimes speak to him by phone. As a result of the civil war there was no direct postal service between Italy and Somalia, so I would have to write to someone in Dubai who would forward the letter to him in Somalia.

While I was away from my homeland the rebel forces finally overturned the corrupt and violent government of Siad Barre. They took Mogadishu in 1990, forcing Siad Barre to flee to Kenya and to Nigeria. One faction proclaimed Ali Mahdi Muhammad president, while another championed Mohamed Farrah Aidid.

The streets of Mogadishu saw some very ugly and violent scenes. In 1992 the United Nations peacekeeping forces began Operation Restore Hope, in which Pakistan, Italy and Malaysia also participated.

In 1991 I was surprised to receive a letter from my girlfriend Ubah, who was now living in London with her family. I had seen little of her since our time in Hargeisa, though she had visited me for a week in Mogadishu once when she had to go there to collect a passport. After that she had gone to live with an uncle in Kuwait. She was now suggesting I join her in England.

In September 1991 I flew to London and found that Ubah had turned into a full-blown woman – very beautiful by Somali standards, even though she was now perhaps a little on the large side for western ideas of beauty. We got on very well, I proposed marriage and we got engaged. But it was very difficult living in separate countries. She didn't have a passport, so she couldn't visit me in Rome.

Our plan to get married was put on hold, though I still hoped it would work out.

Chapter Seven

DOWN AND OUT IN LONDON

After my first visit to London to see Ubah, I thought my future was bright. I was very impressed by England and decided to return there to continue my career as a doctor.

Apart from Ubah being there, I felt a strong connection with Britain. My birthplace had been a British protectorate, and the secondary school where I had discovered my love of learning had been built and staffed by the British Council. Names like Piccadilly Circus and Oxford Street had been familiar to me from my reading and studies since I had been a boy at school. I felt sure I would be at home in Britain.

I arrived in England to stay in mid-December 1992. The weather was chilly and I found London much colder than Rome. As soon as I landed at Heathrow Airport I went to the Home Office in Corydon, the following day, with another Somali and told them I was a refugee direct from Somalia – I never told them I had been studying in Rome for four years. It would be much harder now to get away with that. They told me I could stay for one year initially, which could be extended to four years, and then they would expect me to return as a Somalian citizen as soon as Somalia had a government.

In early 1993, soon after I arrived in the UK, I submitted my primary medical degree and second degree in haematology to be evaluated by the General Medical Council. But to my horror, my registration was turned down. The GMC did not recognise my first degree from the National University of Somalia.

Having done four years training in haematology on top of my first degree in a centre of excellence in haematology, I was expecting to get at least a specialist registrar post. I was even more shocked to find that my classmates who had graduated from the same institute in Italy were allowed to practise even without taking the PLAB examination (Professional and Linguistics Assessment Board). Some of them had difficulty in speaking English.

I thought the GMC's decision to effectively bar non-European doctors like me from practising medicine was unfortunate, to say the least. It set me back a very long way in my career; as it turned out, it would take me nearly fifteen years to get back to where I should have been. The decision left a scar in my mind which has never healed.

To work in the USA I needed refugee status, and I was horrified to find that the UK authorities would not grant this to me. Instead they would only allow me 'Exceptional Leave to Remain'. This meant that I had no status; I was labelled an alien, as if I had green skin and had just landed from Mars. Refugees have rights – they have the right to travel from country to country, to live where they like and to study and work where they like, like a normal citizen. Aliens have very few.

No sooner had this happened than my love life went wrong as

well. The marriage I had hoped for never happened. In my absence in Italy Ubah said she had found another man and had decided to marry him instead. I was very upset, and very angry with her.

These blows left me feeling quite devastated, and the period that followed was the unhappiest of my life. I fell into despair. I could not see any future. I was now homeless, rootless and penniless and had lost my girlfriend, my career and my dignity. To add to my troubles, I learned that my mother, brother and sisters were now in refugee camps in Ethiopia. Fortunately, in early 1993 the information reached me via some contacts in Dubai that they were safe.

I found somewhere to live in Harrow-on-the-Hill for a few weeks before moving into a hostel in Camberwell, Southwark. I stayed in that hostel for the next four years, suffering from depression, unable to sleep or think properly.

My only option seemed to be to study for the USMLE (the United States Medical Licensing Examination). This is a three-step examination for medical licensure in the United States, sponsored by the Federation of State Medical Boards (FSMB) and the National Board of Medical Examiners. The USMLE assesses a physician's ability to apply knowledge, concepts, and principles and to demonstrate the fundamental patient-centered skills that are important in health and disease and constitute the basis of safe and effective patient care. You have to pass all three steps to qualify.

Fortunately my friend Ahmed Abdirahman, who is now a practising doctor in the UK, also lived in Southwark with his family, and I socialised with them regularly. The hostel was near Kings

College Hospital, the big teaching hospital, so when I embarked on my studies for the USMLE I was able to use the library there. I spent hours in the library and read almost every book on medicine it had. In June that year I passed Step One (Basic Medical Science) and began to study for Step Two (Clinical Science).

The hostel was very humble, but it did provide a secure refuge for me. Among the other residents was another Somali refugee, Ali Ismail, a very dynamic individual. He soon decided to go back to Somalia, despite the civil war that was still going on there. He currently lives and works in Hargeisa, Somaliland, with his wife and his two children.

Another Somali, Mohamed Afgoye, an engineer, lived near the hostel with his wife, and I bumped into him while we were doing casual work. He asked me whether I wanted to do some additional work to boost my income. Of course I said yes, so he told me to come back the next morning.

The next day I went back to join Mohamed and we were taken in a white van to a factory in North London where they were manufacturing videotapes. It was like an enormous hangar divided into two areas, one where the tapes were processed and the other where they were put into plastic containers. Most of the workers were women in the processing section. I was then advised to join an employment agency which supplied labour to the factory, and I applied there to do shift work at the factory.

My job was to collect the tapes as they came off the production line and carry them to a trolley. The tapes came off so fast that you often had to carry 20 tapes at once, and you had to be quick.

I usually worked the 7 am to 3 pm shift or the 3 pm to 11 pm shift.

The work was very hard and I would get home each night exhausted. I had never imagined working in such harsh conditions, different from anything I had seen in Somalia, but although it was a back-breaking job it was worth it for the extra money I earned. I was able to use it to buy shoes and clothes for myself. I gave it up after a month, but I went back for three months the following winter, 1995-6.

Britain was now in recession and the economic outlook was gloomy. The Prime Minister, John Major, could not get a grip on the situation. I witnessed Black Wednesday and Britain's withdrawal from the Exchange Rate Mechanism (ERM). Having lived in a country which had been tearing itself apart, I found it extraordinary to watch Britain, such a rich and civilised country and one I had so admired from afar, in such a mess, and the politicians apparently unable to deal with its problems.

People believe British law and British universities are the best in the world and that when you come back from the UK you are sure to have acquired a lot of knowledge. I'm not sure that is really true, but I certainly am grateful for what I have learned in Britain.

In May 1994 I had to apply for a three-year extension to my period of exceptional leave. It felt very uncomfortable being labelled an alien once again, but it was a straightforward enough process to report to the Alien Office to register again. Life continued to revolve around a routine of sleeping, watching TV and taking walks, once in the morning and once in the evening. I was now suffering from very low self-esteem and depression.

One day I walked into the city centre and headed for Trafalgar

Square. In the city I came to a sweet shop. It was the lunch hour and the shop was full of smartly-dressed people. I reached for the sweets I wanted, but as I did so one of the ladies said 'Can I help you?' For some reason I thought they were going to accuse me of shoplifting, and I panicked. Without thinking I just dashed out of the shop. To this day I don't really know why I did that.

On another occasion, in 1995, I bought a book of medicine for a friend of mine who was practising in Somalia, as there were no new books in Somalia. Mohamed Afgoye and I entered W H Smith at Elephant & Castle in Southwark to buy daily papers, and paid for them. A security guard suspected that we had stolen a book from the shop and ran after us. We stopped and asked what was wrong, and he said he thought we might have stolen goods. We were very surprised, as this allegation was totally wrong.

He led us back to the shop. I protested that the book I had was not their book but a medical book, and they did not even sell such books. But the security guard did not listen.

When we entered the shop, I suggested they should scan it. Everybody in the shop was staring at us as if we were criminals. Ultimately a nice lady at the till decided to scan the book, and they realized it was not their book after all. At first they did not even apologize. I realised that there was a manager who was responsible for the problem, and when I challenged him he ultimately told the guard to apologize.

My private studies continued, and in September 1994 I passed Step Two (Clinical Science) of the USMLE. It was easy to brush up my medical knowledge and I was determined. I worked very hard at it, and was delighted to pass all the exams first time.

I also passed the English component, so I started applying for jobs in American hospitals. I was offered several interviews, but all my hopes were dashed when the American Embassy in London refused to grant me a visa to allow me to go to the USA.

Having been granted Exceptional Leave to Remain in the UK was now causing great problems. Refugee status would have enabled me to get a visa. As a failed asylum seeker, I was not eligible for some of the support and benefits that go with refugee status. But this was not the end of the obstacles I had to face. Because of my alien status the US Embassy would not grant me a visa. I applied twice, but was turned down both times.

I had only a travel document which stood for a passport. I was, therefore, able to travel to some countries, and in 1995 I decided to take a holiday in Ethiopia. Although historically Somalia and Ethiopia had fought each other in many wars, the refugees from the north were living in refugee camps in Eastern Ethiopia and in Addis Ababa, the Ethiopian capital.

My trip took me as far as Hargeisa, and it was a fateful visit because it was here that I met my future wife. My best friend Dr Ahmed Abdi, whom I had met in secondary school, ran a pharmacy with his wife Rahma, and working with them was a young woman called Nimo. In the mornings Nimo was working as an auxiliary in a paediatric ward at Hargeisa Group Hospital, and in the afternoons she was working part-time in the pharmacy. Dr Ahmed and Rahma introduced me to her.

Nimo had not been able to finish her schooling because she

had to help her mother, as is traditional in Somali families, which was a shame as she was a very intelligent girl as well as very beautiful. At 25 years old she was quite a bit younger than me. She had done a crash course in pharmacy to satisfy the growing demand in Somalia for pharmacists.

When I met Nimo, it was love at first sight. This time there was no dithering, no delay – I knew almost at once that I wanted to marry her. In fact it was only when I met her that I was finally able to put my hurt over Ubah behind me.

I spent two months in Hargeisa, from July to September 1995, and by the time I left Nimo and I were practically engaged. Of course I could not simply ask her to marry me – it had to be arranged through her family. I told Ahmed of my intentions, he talked to Rahma and she spoke to Nimo. Then I had to ask her parents for her hand in marriage.

I came back to London in October 1995 to raise money for my forthcoming wedding by doing any job available. I returned to Somaliland in early February 1996 for the marriage, which took place in Hargeisa. I did not tell my family about it, although Muse found out and came to the wedding.

The wedding was a very happy occasion. There is a tradition in our culture for the bride's family to present the groom's family with one or more xeedho, which are elaborately-wrapped parcels representing the bride. The xeedho is wrapped and secured very intricately so that it is extremely difficult to open. Inside they pack cured meat preserved in pure locally made ghee, and some of them are later on given to other families. These are returned to the family with gifts of money.

The challenge for the groom, his family and friends is to get the xeedho open without cutting it. It can take days, and in some cases people actually bring in professionals to help them. It took my friends and the men in my family three hours to open our xeedho.

After the marriage, Nimo and I came to Addis Ababa in order to apply for a family reunion at British Embassy in Ethiopia. Unfortunately, the British Embassy in Addis Ababa would not let me take Nimo back to the UK after the wedding because I didn't have a job or a proper place to live. A man called Hassan who was an employee of the British Embassy in Ethiopia demanded a bribe, but all I could afford was a hundred dollars. Of course it was nowhere near enough, as he was demanding around thousand dollars, so I had to return to England without Nimo.

Soon I heard that she was pregnant with our first child, my lovely daughter Muna. I decided to apply for a regular job so that I could bring my family to England.

Good news finally came in 1996 when the GMC finally agreed to recognise my degree from the University of Somalia, which allowed me to sit the PLAB examination. However, I felt I could not wait. I needed to find some sort of regular job as quickly as possible so that I could bring Nimo and little Muna over, so I started looking round for something connected to medicine. I had no experience or qualifications in any other area, and I certainly didn't want to go back to shifting videotapes. The hunt for a better job was on.

Chapter Eight

A JOB IN THE COMMUNITY

One day in the spring of 1997 I spotted an advertisement in The Guardian for a mental health development worker with an organisation called Somali Mental Health. This was a charitable body based in Sheffield which was offering help to people in the local Somali community with mental health difficulties. I applied for the job and was called for an interview.

The chairman of the interview panel was a member of the local Somalian community. The other two members were a Nigerian, Dr Ogo Ossamor, and a lady called Janice Marks, the Honorary Secretary, whom I found to be an exceptional woman; she became a great supporter and friend of mine.

After the interview the chairman said they might call me and offer me something. This seemed to indicate that I wasn't going to get the job that was on offer. However, a couple of weeks later the phone rang and it was the chairman. He said they had decided to offer me a three-month trial because of my experience in psychiatry. Their letter said they had been 'most impressed by the knowledge, skills and experience' I had shown during my interview, which made me feel much better.

The work involved seeing people in the community who were in need of mental health services. There are around 4000 Somalis in Sheffield, of a total of 100,000 in the UK, so there was a lot of demand for our help.

Mental health care for the Somali community is quite an issue. Even when living in England, first-generation Somalis usually turn to the local sheikhs, the spiritual healers, before they resort to conventional medicine, because they assume a person who is behaving oddly is possessed by evil spirits, like the girl I encountered back in Aluula. When they came to us they would be suffering from all the mental conditions associated with the stresses of life – depression, schizophrenia and other enduring mental illness of various kinds. The British-born generation are westernised, but their parents still cling to the old traditions and beliefs.

Somali Mental Health gave me a great deal of support from the outset. After the first three months they extended the term to six months, and then they made it permanent. In the end, I stayed there for nearly ten years.

I soon got into a routine. Each day I would first visit a few patients in hospital, the Northern General Hospital in Sheffield, to help them sort out any problems they had. For example, they might not be claiming their due benefit, or I might need to liaise with the community psychiatric nurse or social worker about their care. Some of them needed housing sorted out. In some cases I would arrange appeals against sectioning, in collaboration with their solicitor. In addition to having mental health problems they often could not speak much English, so they might need me to act as an interpreter. Some of them would have been out on the streets if we had not been there to help them.

The Somali patients were usually on one of the two psychiatric wards at the hospital. If they were not on an open ward, for their own safety they might be kept on a low-secure unit or a medium-secure unit for the more seriously ill. Any dangerous or highly disturbed people who were of risk to others were sent to high-security places like Rampton and Broadmoor.

Although I found some of the work harrowing, it was not all doom and gloom. I found it very rewarding to see someone you have helped walking the streets as a full member of society. That's when you feel you have achieved something. And during my later years at Somali Mental Health I was able to play a significant role in two very successful conferences on mental health.

Somali Mental Health gave me compassionate leave to bring my family over and paid me a generous extra sum to cover the expense. Nimo was able to join me in October 1998 and we moved into a two-bedroom flat. Soon she was pregnant again, with another daughter. We called her Najma, which means star, and indeed she is a real star.

I was happy at first in my new post, but it was a terrible struggle for Nimo because she was at home bringing up the children in a country where she had none of her friends or family to turn to and did not know the language. That meant I had to run all our domestic affairs and take the family shopping early in the morning before I went to work. I soon found that the salary of £21,000 was not enough to support a growing family. I bitterly regretted not being able to practise as a doctor as I felt I should have been allowed to do.

The truth is, I had probably developed depression soon after I arrived in London and encountered so many barriers to pursuing my career. I thought I would be happy once I had Nimo with me, but life proved very challenging for both of us and was not working out at all as I had expected. I began to feel tired, irritable and very worried about the future. I did not sleep well or eat properly and my self-esteem and confidence had become very low. Sometimes I would lose interest in everything. I even developed irritable bowel syndrome because of the constant feelings of anxiety.

Finally I went to see my GP, who prescribed Paroxetine, an antidepressant for a trial. Unfortunately this badly affected my sex life, so I stopped taking the tablets after a couple of weeks. I tried another antidepressant which was no better than the first, so from then on I decided to manage without drugs.

My mood began to fluctuate and I experienced periods of intense irritability and anger, as well as many days of gloom. This went on for several long and difficult years, during which I continued to feel unable to return to my ambition of qualifying as doctor in the UK. I suffered from lack of confidence, low self-esteem, and a general inability to cope. Although the Somali Mental Health team were always very kind to me and made me feel valued in the post, it was too long to be doing the same job, and I felt myself becoming stale and bored with the same routine week after week.

However I took great comfort from my growing family. Two very bright boys, Ibrahim and Ismail, followed our girls, which brought us great joy. It was in 2005, when Nimo became pregnant with Ismail, that I decided I really had to find a way of getting back into medicine.

That year I finally summoned up the willpower and confidence to sit the PLAB examinations I needed to practise in the UK. I decided to do it in secret as I didn't want any extra pressure from people wondering whether I had passed or not.

I sat the first paper, the theoretical one, in September 2005 and the practical paper in January 2006. I passed them both first time. In March 2005 I went on to pass the ILTS exam which deals with the language aspects. At last, after a gap of 14 years, I was fully qualified to return to my career as a doctor.

However, the timing was not good. A new European directive had just forced the Department of Health to reduce the number of hours doctors could work from 80 to 48. By lowering the bar they solved that problem, but they opened the floodgates. Thousands of immigrant doctors applied for jobs and the competition was fierce. After all the years of waiting, I began to wonder if I would ever fulfil my ambition of practising as a psychiatrist in the west.

Chapter Nine

RECOGNITION AT LAST

Finding a medical post was even more of a challenge, as I had not practised medicine since 1992. I needed a clinical attachment, so I wrote to the consultants I had got to know through Somali Mental Health to say I was trying to restart my career and needed help. I got an appointment to see a consultant, and he said he would find an attachment for me, but the one they offered was in haematology. I turned this down as I wanted to stick with psychiatry. I knew I could do far more with that than with haematology.

I was helped by an organisation called the Highly Skilled Migrant Programme, which supports professionally-qualified people from overseas and helps them to find work. The Labour government had put aside some money for doctors to be retrained, and in South Yorkshire and Humberside Deanery they had money for five posts. I was one of 10 candidates who applied for them.

One Monday morning a few days after the interview, I was feeling very low and not at all optimistic about getting a job. Then the phone rang and it was a woman from the Deanery. 'Congratulations!' she said. 'We are offering you a psychiatric post.' I was delighted, and very relieved.

Nimo was very happy at this news. It was a big turning point for the family after so many years of poverty, struggling and frustration. Somali Mental Health were sad to see me go, but they understood that I had been a long time in the same job and they were very pleased that I had at last got my wish to become a doctor in Britain. The manager, Saeed Abdi, who has become a long-standing friend, wrote in my reference letter 'He worked hard and with unfailing dedication to help the Somali community to access services and worked with the local community mental health teams to deliver appropriate culturally-sensitive service. His rich experience in culture and diversity is a boon to all who come into contact with him or need his support.'

They asked me to find a consultant who could have me for four months, and I was able to get a placement with Dr Simon Mullins. From November to February 2007 I was with Sheffield Crisis Team, which is based in its own unit serving the area around the city. I was working as a pre-registration house officer.

Five days into my placement I received an urgent phone call from my brother who told me that my mother was seriously ill. She was taken to Hargeisa group hospital, where unfortunately she passed away the following day. It was very sad that she died just as I had finally got what I had been working for so many years.

Hargeisa Hospital is the biggest hospital in Somaliland and was built by the British when Somaliland was British protectorate. The hospital is old and lacks modern facilities to manage acutely-ill patients. People with serious problems such as heart attack have no chance of survival.

At the end of my placement, I was asked to do an audit and a 360-degree appraisal to assess my abilities. I was successful, and they put me on the locum register. This was great news.

I went on the books of a medical agency called NHS Professionals and the first job they found me was at Stockport Hospital in north-east Cheshire. I was only there for a very short time. I did a week of nights there, then days, and then from March to August 2007 I worked in Walton Hospital Chesterfield, Derbyshire, under the supervision of Dr John Sykes. Dr Sykes is a Consultant in Old Age Psychiatry and the Medical Director of Derbyshire Mental Health Foundation Trust. He is an excellent consultant with an enormous ability to listen and take into account the opinions of other staff before reaching a rational decision. In this way he is just like a chief in an African tribe.

What I really wanted was a training post, but I was not successful. Because so many doctors failed to get posts in mid 2007, the Government decided that all deaneries should interview the doctors who failed to get jobs. However it was all a charade, because they had already selected the people they wanted. The Government forced them to hold the interviews, but they were only going through the motions.

Derbyshire Mental Health then offered me a three-month post in Matlock to fill in for a doctor who had taken a three-month sabbatical, but after I had been there a month NHS Professionals came back to me and said they wanted me to go and work for a month in Barrow-in-Furness in Cumbria. I had never heard of Cumbria, let alone Barrow-in-Furness. Later on the agency told me it would be extended to six months, which made more sense. They found me a room in the little town of Millom, on the coast, which seemed to be quite close to Barrow as the crow flies.

I needed a car for this, so I bought an old Nissan Micra. The journey from Sheffield to Millom was 270 miles, and it took me the whole day to get there. I lost my way on a number of occasions. Millom turned out to be on the other side of an estuary from Barrow, so I had to follow a winding road around the coast, which was very difficult after dark.

But when I finally saw the scenery in daylight, I was very impressed. Cumbria was a beautiful area, and it even reminded me of the area around Sheikh in the rainy season. The hills were rugged and green and the roads were as narrow and winding as the mountain passes back home. Barrow, however, turned out to be a very deprived area; it reminded me of Sheffield.

There was a very experienced consultant at Furness General Hospital, Dr Anthony Page, a graduate from Leeds, now retired. I started with a three-day induction in Kendal. The work itself was not difficult and I was getting £30 an hour, which was more than I had ever earned before. I used to stay in the hospital in Barrow when I was doing on call, sometimes for 72 hours at a time to save the travelling. I was looking after patients in two acute psychiatry general wards.

When I had time off I visited the main lakes, Windermere and Coniston. I thought Windermere and its scenery were amazing. I took a boat trip along the lake, which reminded me of my first experience in a boat, returning from Aluula, though it was more civilised and the water was much calmer.

Later on I moved from Millom to Barrow in order to be nearer to the hospital where I worked. This time I stayed with two friends of mine, Jean and Steve Skelton, who lived in a wonderful house. Both were highly experienced nurses who had been helping people with mental health problems all their lives. They were indeed a wonderful couple. I cannot forget their generosity and hospitality.

In Cumbria I gained experience with patients suffering from all kinds of mental illness, including schizophrenia, depression, bipolar disorder and anxiety disorder. I worked there until the following June, 2008, when I applied for a staff grade job. I worked as a locum at Highbury Hospital, Nottingham, for a month, and then in August 2008 I went to Sheffield to take on a Senior House Officer-level post in old age psychiatry at the Longley Centre. This was a training post. After that I did a year working for Dearne Valley Community Mental Health Trust based in Barnsley, in the community psychiatric unit. In February 2010 I became a speciality trainee registrar with the Assertive Outreach Team at Derby Mental Health Service.

Mental illness is a terrible problem in this country, and a very expensive one because it puts people out of work for so long, perhaps the rest of their lives. We waste people because they can't get a job. It's a vicious circle. Not being able to get a job makes you depressed, and because you are depressed and have low self-esteem you don't have the confidence to look for work. It can destroy people. I know what that feels like from personal experience. The Government has put a lot of money into surgery, neurology, and other medical disciplines, but mental illness is still, as they say, the Cinderella of health care.

By now my career was going well, but in fairness to Nimo it was difficult for me to be away from home so much. For almost five years she had to take the children to and from school twice a day - she still does. Last year she started a diploma course in childcare, which she will finish in May 2012. Besides doing her studies and looking after the children, she works as a carer. Muna is a wonderful daughter and is very helpful to her mother, and her younger sister Najma is very good to us as well.

Many times on cold winter days in Sheffield we think of the sunshine we left behind in Somalia. We still miss the familiar streets and people, the trees and the hills. Somalis who have been here for many years always talk of going back, perhaps retiring to their old country, though they rarely do it - certainly not the younger generation who were born here. Those who do go back soon change their minds when they discover once again how poor and difficult life is there.

Nimo does miss her homeland, and I think if it hadn't been for the children she might have wanted to go back, but they are well settled now and very happy in their community.

My children went back for a visit to Somalia with Nimo two years ago. They were able to see their grandparents on Nimo's side of the family. The two girls liked the country, but Ismael was only four and didn't enjoy it much. Ibrahim, who was nine, didn't like the food, because he has been a vegetarian since he was small. He decided early on that he did not like the taste of meat or fish.

Here is a report by Muna and Najma about their trip:

'We were very excited at the thought of going back to our homeland at first, until we realised that we would have to take plenty of vaccinations to be able to go. But our excitement at going overrode our fears about the vaccinations.

'The next big hurdle to overcome was the almighty journey that we had to take. First of all was our five-hour trip down to Heathrow. We rented a car and left at midnight on the night of our flight. A family friend drove us to London with our entire luggage. The moment we heard the sounds of aeroplanes taking off and landing, the excitement of going on an aeroplane was overwhelming. When we boarded the Royal Brunei Airlines plane it took us a bit of time to get use to the environment, because the first flight took eight hours to get to Dubai. But the air hostesses kept us entertained.

'When we got into Dubai the high temperature was a bit much. It was as if the heaters had been turned up too high and sometimes it felt as though we were suffocating. The hotel we stayed at was fairly reasonable. Our mum told us we weren't allowed to go out in the daytime because it was too hot, but we had the chance to stroll around at night because it was cooler. We spent two days in Dubai before taking a two-hour flight to Djibouti, and then it was a short journey to Hargeisa.

'The cool breeze of Hargeisa caught our attention immediately. It kept the temperature bearable. But what was nicer was the group of people waiting to greet us after our long travels. The two months we spent in Hargeisa were amazing. We went to the mosque on Fridays, visited our grandparents' house a lot of the time, went to the countryside and visited two of their best hotels. We got used to family life. Every day ended with us, our cousins, our aunty and our housemaids sitting around the small TV for an hour to watch a film before going to bed.

'We had visits and we went on visits, but what was more important was that it became home for us. The heavy rainfall kept the temperature steady. The fun our family and friends gave us kept us entertained. Our trip to Hargeisa was unbeatable and unforgettable and we all still long to go back there.'

I would like to visit Somalia again myself, but while I am working as a locum I cannot afford to take the time off. I might consider it if I get a staff grade job with paid holidays. Nimo does miss her family. They are a much stronger and closer family than mine, and of course she lived with them until she was grown up, while I left when I was only a boy. One day we may want to retire to Somalia, although we do not even have a plot of land there yet.

We don't discuss the difficult years when I was so depressed and life for both of us was such a struggle. I have the satisfaction of knowing that the little money I earned was invested in my children, who are a joy to us every day of our lives.

There are moments of gloom sometimes when I remember the past and what I had to go through to escape from the poverty of Somalia and practise as a doctor in the west. I must remember that there are many doctors from Somalia just like me who do not have jobs and have no real prospect of ever working here as doctors.

I still worry about the problems in my homeland. Somalia is

still a patchwork country, with no central government since 1991. The north at least is relatively stable as the self-declared, but unrecognized, sovereign state of Somaliland. The Islamist Al-Shabaab movement controls a large part of the south of the country, and has imposed a strict and brutal régime based on sharia law. I feel that it's the West, led by the USA, that created Al-Shabaab. I certainly don't regret not having gone to the USA to work.

Somalia has a very bad name internationally because of the constant unrest there and the upsurge in piracy, which is only a result of great poverty, but I still love my country and hope it will become a more peaceful place again before too long.

In the meantime I'm happy with my wife and children here in the UK, and looking forward to whatever life has in store for us next.

* * * * * * * *

ND - #0126 - 270225 - C0 - 234/156/6 - PB - 9781909020047 - Matt Lamination